unlock your business voice

how to **speak** as well as you **think**

Simon de Cintra

RETHINK PRESS

First published in Great Britain 2018
by Rethink Press (www.rethinkpress.com)

Cartoons by Andrew Priestley

For my daughter Alexandria – you studied while I wrote and we both #GSD.

CONTENTS

PART **4**
YOUR REPEAT VOICE PRESCRIPTION

Preface

I cannot name a single profession, job or role in society that does not require us all to have the confidence and skills to be heard. We are in the Communication Age, online and offline. How we deliver a message and the skills to gain engagement are as critical as the content we deliver. In fact, I would like to be brave enough to say, how we deliver the message, our voice, is more important than the words we use.

Simon de Cintra's fascinating career has enabled him to share both his experience and the science behind his message to enable the reader to move forwards with such empathy and gentle teachings. His desire to help us all become 'the best version of ourselves' is clear in his generous study and sharing. In his words, we must have a 'credible voice'. Our skills to engage in all interactions we have, whether we are networking, public speaking, pitching for investment, in a meeting with one or more people, even online, will determine our success. How we enter a room, deliver our message and manage conflict all have an impact.

We say we are in a 'Knowledge Economy'. Our knowledge is only part of our success in a time when our skills to engage, build trust and communicate effectively will determine whether others truly listen and are influenced by our beliefs.

We have a choice in life, to fit in, to go with the crowd or, as Simon says, 'dare to be different'. We must be brave and have opinions and deliver them with credibility. Many brilliant people have not been heard, despite their relentless speaking, networking and writing, and this will undoubtedly be because they are not delivering their thoughts with the skills required to influence the audience in an overwhelming world of communication and information.

I have loved reading Simon's book. As a writer, public speaker and entrepreneur, I have experienced resistance, fear, anxiety and failure. Simon's book will sit by my side; his metaphors, practical exercises, case studies and tips have had a powerful impact on me and I will refer to his book many times before important meetings and speaking engagements. This is not a book to read just once; I am sure, like me, readers will highlight and make notes and return again and again to its profound lessons.

Each of us have an opportunity to be 'the best version of ourselves', but this cannot be done without acknowledgement of our skills, weaknesses and a determination to keep working on certain aspects of our ability to achieve the results we need to achieve our life goals. Communication is without doubt a joy or a challenge for us all. I can categorically say that my ability to communicate has been one of my joys; it is quite possibly the key factor in my own progress, but I also know I can improve and it feels good to know how.

Penny Power OBE
Entrepreneur, Speaker and Writer
CEO The Business Cafe

Foreword

Communication is at the very core of human life. From the day we are born we are communicating, with smiles, frowns, laughter, crying and body language. As we grow and mature, the way we communicate evolves and adapts, but its fundamental role in shaping every aspect of our lives remains just as prominent.

The art of effective communication is so critical in this modern, ever inclusive world, with the need to connect and engage effectively across countries, languages, religion, ages, gender and more. In addition to this, empathy in modern business and society has increasingly taken centre stage in recent years, along with the understanding that to get the best from people, you need to treat them as they like to be treated.

As technology and innovation progress, more ways of communicating will emerge, with digital innovation supporting this evolutionary process and making cross-cultural communication even easier. Translation technology is already well established and people are becoming more aware of the need to acknowledge other views, cultures and experiences. If you think change is fast now, it is only going to get faster in the future!

Millennials, in particular, are facilitating this rapid pace of change, transforming the 'traditional' world of work as we used to know it and causing organisations to re-evaluate the way they operate in order to remain productive, profitable and keep hold of their best talent. Millennial employees are highly communicative, agile and highly accountable. For them, purpose is more important than profitability.

The word 'purpose' has never been more important for either organisations or their respective business leaders. Purpose defines the reason why a firm, and indeed a person, exists; it directly affects the impact and legacy they will leave on others and on society. Everyone has their purpose – something Simon alludes to in this book through his discussion of knowing your 'casting'. Understanding the role and position you play in a business can only come from knowing your purpose.

This shift in mindset is proving a challenge to many organisations. In business it is all too easy to let short term greed rule over doing the right thing for the long term. But the latter is necessary for survival in the marketplace of the future. 'Business in the community' and the idea of being a force for good is gaining momentum, with honest and transparent communication playing a huge part in this new and exciting way of working. The work I'm personally involved in with Business in the Community, The Prince's Responsible Business Network, promotes and supports businesses to be responsible, resilient and sustainable. This includes how employees and supply chain behave, with transparency an essential deliverable. But transparency is rarely a given in business, often as a result of poor communication skills at various levels.

Too often in business we have to fix problems that have happened because of a breakdown in communication, either due to different views of the truth or because a someone said everything was OK when it wasn't. When faced with different versions of the truth, it is critical that business leaders ensure that everyone understands and agrees to the same terms and intentions, whilst also understanding the differences in opinions, views and experiences. It's about being aware of your own 'DNA' and background and being prepared to make allowances for differences in others to boost collaboration and ensure that any conflict is of a healthy nature. It's about being transparent, empowered and accountable.

In his popular TEDx talk, highly renowned public speaking expert Richard Greene spoke about the importance of not just giving a 'speech' but rather creating 'conversations' from the heart. This is at the core of authentic communication, but doesn't necessarily mean everything has to be 'nice'.

Fairness underpins my leadership position and approach. The ability to have a fair and transparent conversation about performance without being expected to be nice is critical. Fair conversations ensure that any issues are aired and addressed before it is too late and the all important trust is broken. Fairness is born out of trust and integrity, the desire to genuinely help a colleague to improve and not to avoid what some may describe as a difficult conversation. If your intentions are honourable and positive and you really want to help, you must be fair rather than nice.

The concept of fairness, learning and moving on, taking responsibility for our own communication and actions and most importantly adapting our style to the needs of the specific environment and situation, are absolutely key to succeeding in modern day working life. Through writing this book, Simon has skillfully put the 'workbook' element of this theory into context and, critically, into the real world of work.

Unlock Your Business Voice is there to support anyone who needs to communicate more effectively in business. Many people are experts in the art of communicating at work; for most it did not come naturally and was not achieved without significant investment in self-development. Like all things in business, practice makes perfect!

I encourage you to read the book, learn, then practise. Then practise some more. The more you practise, the better you will get. Spend time with as many different people, ask good questions, tell good stories and observe others, to understand the things they do well and how they do it.

If you are a 'Driver' like me, you may want to skim the chapters, do a few exercises to get some results and then go to the repeat prescription at the end, picking the book back up for a booster from time to time. Others will enjoy the stories and the references to the research that backs up the techniques, as well as the practical hints and tips.

Whatever your motivation for picking up this book, by the end I have no doubt that you will have gained a greater understanding of how to interpret the business world around you, how to unlock your business voice and how to communicate fairly, authentically and with true purpose.

Mike Still

Mike has over 30 years of experience in the insurance and risk management industry, including 12 years as a Managing Director at Marsh and prior to that Aon. As well his corporate career, Mike has always cared passionately about making a difference to people, businesses and communities. Mike is currently Chair of HRH The Prince of Wales' Business Emergency Resilience Group; and Trustee, Director and Scottish Chair of Business in the Community. www.bitc.org.uk

Introduction

Have you ever sat in a meeting with your inner voice in overdrive, burning to share that killer concept you've so ingeniously cooked up, only for the moment to be stolen by somebody else pipping you to the post? If and when you do get the chance to speak, do you get lost in the detail before you can dispatch the golden nugget? I wish I'd had this book to read twenty years ago when I was beginning to build my career as it contains the advice I'm still self-administering today.

The VOICE Methodology has practical steps and exercises that will help bridge the knowing and doing gap that may be holding you back right now. The good news is that it's not a long-winded or time-consuming process. I'm sure you're already busy enough; I will help you to be more effective in your communications so that you can focus on business rather than 'busy-ness'. The 'how you say it' isn't just in the performance; it's as much about the structure and order you design into your message. Everyone's looking for the hook.

My first piece of advice would be: beware of your cognitive biases. There are a few that can get in the way of you speaking as well as you think, for instance the idea that only actors, singers and performers have great voices. Everyone has a great voice; the insight comes from accepting the relationship between thought, breath and action. Dialling the inner voice down will help you to dial your business voice up.

That's my headline concept. This book isn't about flicking a switch as that would risk you becoming inauthentic, which goes against the key to credible business voices. It's a question of small adjustments that will help you flex your communication style to suit your audience.

The simple five-step process – VOICE – can easily be carried in your head. It's like a portable drive that's always with you, plugged in ready to go. From now on, you'll never be without your VOICE:

- **V**ocation – being understood by others is more important than being the expert in your own head
- **O**bservation – people learn most easily from watching others at work
- **I**ntention – making deliberate choices about the effect you want to have on others will dramatically increase the chances of getting what you want

- **C**asting – add skills and techniques to make the authentic you more compelling to others, adapting your style, not your personality
- **E**xperiment – have the courage to get things wrong, reflect, improve and move on to discover your most effective communication style

By following my VOICE Methodology, you will learn a practical and simple approach to increasing your competence and confidence in business communication, whether it's a one to one conversation or speaking to hundreds at an industry conference. The principles are the same irrespective of the situation. I've had plenty of experience in helping people so I know that my methodology works.

There are people in business whom others listen to intently, buying into their ideas and acting upon them. Have you ever noticed that the ones who do command the attention of an audience sometimes have little to say, or that their thoughts are not always the most original or insightful? Nevertheless, there's something about the way their message is ordered and delivered that makes it compelling to the audience. It's tempting to think it's purely instinctive; that these people are born with the gift of the gab and it's everyone else's fate to work much harder to be heard, understood and persuasive.

It doesn't have to be this way. Now it's your time to unlock the potent business voice in your head and be listened to. It's your turn to be the one people will want to hear. Please allow me to help you.

In business, the days of all sizzle and no substance are definitely on the ropes. The fastest growing businesses are high tech, either directly through their product ecosystems or indirectly by what is driving exponential growth. Whichever way you look at it, the age of the Expert Introvert is now truly upon us.

The demands placed on the technical expert are significant. The challenge is to get your ideas out of your head and into the arena, speaking as well as you think during project team, senior leadership and board level briefings. An empowered business voice will help you move your business forward and ensure your expertise and creativity (introverts have creativity in bucket loads) are used for everyone's benefit and reward. You just need to have belief in yourself and know how to use it.

During our working lives, we strive to assimilate the knowledge, expertise and experience that will make us credible in our chosen field. This process is often challenging and will involve sacrifices, commitment and plain old putting the hours in. Quite rightly, we feel a sense of achievement when we get the recognition our efforts deserve, from graduation day to entry into professional bodies; from getting that big break job offer to being promoted. It's not surprising, therefore, that the opposite is also true. When we can't leverage what we've worked so hard to attain, we're naturally going to feel frustrated and deflated.

Today's world of business spins so fast. If we don't hook the other brains in the room quickly into our way of thinking, then what sounded so clear and compelling in our own head won't get airtime. Our business voice will remain unheard. The transfer of ideas doesn't happen by telepathy, so we need the rest of our business machine, i.e. our body and voice, to join in.

During twenty-five years in business, I have coached and mentored subject matter experts who've needed to make more of an impact. My corporate career started in sales, latterly leading the Corporate Card team at American Express. This was where I realised I was more interested in helping introverts become confident in their communication than increasing the amount of plastic in people's wallets.

Over the last ten years, I have led nearly 1,000 workshops all over the world for major organisations as well as at leading business schools. Consequently, I have had the pleasure of working with thousands of highly intelligent people.

Two questions I'm frequently asked are 'Can you really learn this stuff?' and 'How long does it take?' Happily, the answer to the first is a resounding yes, and it doesn't take as long as you may think. Making a few small changes and actually talking less will quickly result in better outcomes and increase the potency of your communication.

Before we explore the VOICE Methodology in more detail, I want to reassure you on a couple of points, particularly, 'Does it actually work in practice?'

While I was at school, my passion was for Chemistry, and I went on to read it at university. I remember being struck by the revelation that in science, all you can do is observe behaviours and characteristics, mould a predictive model around them, and then wait for someone else to spot an anomaly and disprove your hypothesis. That's as good as being an eminent scientist gets!

Later, after a brief brush with the military and my time in financial services, I had a career change (or an early mid-life crisis as some of my friends called it) and went to drama school to retrain as an actor. I was taken by the head of the school's opening address.

'If you think you've come here to learn to act, you're wrong. People won't pay to see you act.'

Thankfully, he didn't add, 'Fame costs, and right here's where you start paying.' Instead, he went on to clarify that what the audience is expecting is a truthful representation of someone else's character and their communication style. That's why there needs to be a process and work involved.

So even though my background has been a mixture of the sciences and arts, both disciplines have taught me to search for the methodology and process behind the result. Consequently, I've spent the last ten years absorbing what others have had to say on the subject, from Albert Mehrabian's often misinterpreted studies on feelings and attitude in the 1960s, to the present day research of Amy Cuddy on stereotyping and discrimination, emotions, power and nonverbal behaviour. I've combined this with keen observation and note-taking while working with talented individuals who wanted to be heard and understood. I'm looking forward to sharing my favourite pieces of research and observation throughout the book. However, I'd like to start our work together with a personal story.

How the VOICE Methodology saved me from bravado

A few years ago, I was hired to deliver a keynote speech at a conference for 800 employees of a global retail brand. The subject was leadership communication, and it needed to link to the new company values and behaviours that were to be launched earlier in the day.

During the preconference briefings, I'd been warned that there may be some cynicism under the banner of 'we've heard this all before' around the new model, so I decided to deliver the first five minutes of my session in an equally cynical tone, Jack Dee style. In the weeks leading up to the conference, which was being held at a beach resort not far from Barcelona, all went well and the outline of my speech, my slides and sample videos were approved by the organisers. I was offered the opportunity to rehearse at the venue the day before the conference, and although that meant missing out on a day's work and finding a stand-in for another workshop I had been due to deliver, I readily accepted.

Thank goodness I did, because at the rehearsal, not all of what had felt and sounded so right in the detachment of my head worked. Even though there could only have been twenty or so watching the rehearsal, I could tell from their reaction that I needed to make changes to fit the audience that would subsequently fill the auditorium.

The preparation I had done up to that point was certainly not wasted; the overall premise, structure and the majority of the content of the speech were all still intact after the rehearsal. What needed work was how my delivery would get the assembled management team to embrace and champion the values and behaviours the company wanted them to adopt. After all, that was the whole point of my session. I gave more thought to the dynamics of the space and how 800 people needed to be guided through the message, and I could only reach this insight by getting it a bit 'wrong'. Working out in advance that my business voice wouldn't have been as effective as I had imagined gave me the opportunity to do something about it.

Walking out of the rehearsal, I resolved to put into practice what I'd been preaching to others over the years and not to let my training as a performer deceive me into thinking that all would 'be alright on the night'. It was the reflective geek inside me that encouraged me to rework the process and be thankful for the opportunity to do so, rather than be wounded by what hadn't worked. This was the '*Eureka*' moment for me, when I first discovered My Business Voice Methodology® by asking myself the following questions during a long walk along the beach.

VOCATION	**Why had I been hired as an external speaker?**
	To add credibility to the new values and behaviours and deal with any cynicism
OBSERVATION	**What tips could I take from other speakers that would match the brief?**
	Set up the story (Hans Rosling), be clear on the message (Sheryl Sandberg) and add a bit of healthy cynicism (Jack Dee)
INTENTION	**What did I need to achieve?**
	Bring the new values to life for 800 people in a simple, engaging and 'grown up' way
CASTING	**How did I want to come across and where would my credibility sit with the audience?**
	The '3 Cs': Certain, Clear and Confident! My authority would come from making the connection early by getting the audience to join me in some simple exercises. Most of all, not be too 'needy'.
EXPERIMENT	**How would I know if my ideas would work in practice?**
	Get them out of my head and into the space by practising out loud and trusting my judgement as to how they'd sound to the audience. I easily found private spaces around the hotel to do this.

At this stage, it didn't really matter if I came up with the perfect answers. Most important was that I believed and was prepared to commit to them. This gave me the scaffolding to frame and build the content.

I went back to the hotel, found an empty meeting room and tried a few things out.

The following day, I built rapport with the crowd and my message hit home. The breakout sessions that followed ran smoothly because everyone was onside. Most importantly, I avoided that awful feeling that any speaker dreads when we know the audience isn't with us, the whole thing can't end soon enough and the opportunity is missed.

The time I'd spent implementing the VOICE Methodology paid off.

Feel free to dip in and out of this book. It's written in a non-preachy and logical order that will give you time to think, reflect, breathe and practise. Keep it within easy reach – it's an invaluable First Aid kit for all your communication ailments.

PART 1

**Get Your Voice
Out In
The Space**

CHAPTER 1

Taking Control Of Your Inner Monologue

"Whether you think you can, or you think you can't – you're right."

HENRY FORD

This wisdom is simplistic and yet irritatingly true.

Before we start looking at the practicalities of unlocking our business voice, let's examine the self-sabotaging mind games people often play on themselves.

Do you ever find yourself ruminating on these thoughts?

- It can be difficult to break into discussions during meetings
- The message is clear in my head, but I lose confidence when I hear myself speak

- Sometimes I sense people wanting me to hurry up
- Self-belief and confidence can nosedive when I sense conflict
- Others' higher status can get in the way of what I'm trying to say

If you responded yes to all five, don't panic. The vast majority of people would say the same. Likewise, if your answer to all five statements was 'It depends', that's perfectly valid, too.

These beliefs are voiced by our inner monologue and fuelled by the reptilian part of our brain – the oldest, most primeval portion of our hard drive. It's responsible for the out-of-body experience we feel when we lose our train of thought and the fight or flight response is triggered during a speech, presentation or high stakes meeting.

If this happens to you, how long do you feel the experience goes on? In my classes, most people tell me it feels like an uncomfortably long time. Yet, very often if we ask the same question of a colleague who was present, their experience will have been different. They'll say the moment passed in an instant, and they're not just being nice about it. There's a physiological reason for this.

You may well recognise the triggers: your heart rate soars through the roof; you feel flushed or go red; and most significantly, your breathing goes haywire and it can feel like you're hyperventilating. If you feel this happening, don't be defeated by it – it's a natural part of being human. Instead, do something about it. Place the palm of your hand on your diaphragm (the part of your chest that moves up and down when you laugh) and take a deep, indulgent breath. Exhale as slowly as possible without straining, and then crucially allow the next breath to arrive naturally. Don't even think about it, just let it happen. This ten-second 'time out' will slow down your heart rate, refuel your voice and switch your consciousness back on.

Remember, you alone are in control of your breathing, not the situation nor anyone else in the room at the time. Think of it in these terms: if you ring your IT helpline, what's often the first thing they tell you to do? Usually, it's 'Turn your computer off and then back on again.' Try the simple things first; they can often solve the problem.

Taking control of our breathing is actually the reverse of what most of us do during moments of stress. Instead, we panic breathe, which triggers the thumping-heart-in-mouth feeling, thereby feeding the flames rather than fighting them.

We also need some internal reprogramming in our level of self-belief. We need to convince ourselves, first and foremost, that we're worth listening to. Even if everything else is working, such as the quality of our insight, the evidence to back up our idea and the structure of our narrative, if the delivery of the message isn't congruent in terms of voice and body, then the recipient won't buy into it and we'll end up working much harder to convince them.

The world of work today has never been so demanding. The American military gave us the acronym VUCA, which stands for 'volatile, uncertain, complex and ambiguous', and this has been adopted by many companies to describe the challenges of doing business in modern times. Yet this can be a highly stimulating and rewarding environment in which to plough our careers. The consequence of this rate of change in business is that there's no shortage of ideas, but there's a very real shortage of time to make strategic decisions. It's somewhat ironic that amongst all the noise around 'big data', more and more key decisions need to be made instinctively.

Like never before, if we've got something worth saying, the right time to say it is right now.

This is where our inner voice can sometimes be behind the times. It wants us to wait until our ideas are fully formed and utterly bulletproof, so that when others hear them, we'll get an immediate green light and off we'll go. Life doesn't work like that. Other people's inner voices aren't necessarily following the same script as ours, and the truth is that decision makers make decisions with other decision makers. The first decision we need to make is to fully back ourselves and accept that the commercial world can't afford to wait for perfection.

That can be an uncomfortable concept for deep thinkers, who like to reflect and refine before demanding airtime. The antidote for this unease is to commit to becoming as clear and confident about what we don't know as what we do.

Have you noticed that senior leaders don't burden themselves with having to know everything? They are confident saying, 'I don't know about that in detail. What I do know is this...' That's an assertive way of communicating. Notice the use of the word 'assertive' rather than 'aggressive'. They are in fact mutually exclusive, and this is an extremely important point of clarification.

Over the years of working with talented people, I've noticed that they often have an issue with their internal settings not matching their external output. Put more practically, they can sound to themselves like they're almost shouting, when the audience think they're only just audible. The same is true regarding the pace of people's speech. Intellectuals have a tendency to race through what they're saying, because it's the natural speed at which they think. The issue to remember is that the recipient of information needs time to process it.

This necessity to reset our inner dials can also be evident in respect of the effect we're trying to have on others when we speak. The impact we have, or don't have, on them and the way we leave them feeling is driven by the decisions we make. Our mind, breathing, voice and body work as an integrated system; we're designed that way, and under normal conditions, it looks after itself without us even thinking about it. This is evident during relaxed conversations, socially or at work. When the trust level is high, we rarely get the response, 'What do you mean by that?' This response only seems to happen when subconsciously we're unclear about our intention, often because we expect the content to do the work alone.

When we don't make conscious decisions about the effect we want our communication to have, the recipient fills in the gap and may well misinterpret how we want them to feel. That's why making choices around intention is so central to unlocking our business voice. Do we want to educate, challenge or inspire our public? Think about doing all three.

People aren't nearly as interested in us as we think. There's a misconception that others are continually judging us and scrutinising what we have to say. In reality, they don't have enough time or energy for this. We get noticed when we merit other people's attention, hopefully for the right reasons. Our focus needs to be on creating the hooks by which we will earn people's attention (rather than attempting to demand it), and then being easy to follow once we've achieved this.

Be generous in sharing your thoughts and hard-won insights. Never forget to switch from broadcast to receive mode during what must always be a two-way process, even when you're delivering a speech.

In conclusion, your inner voice is helpful. It can save you from appearing foolish, so take notice of it. However, just like your external voice, it needs managing. Always be mindful that what you're saying to yourself is transmitted into what you're saying to others.

- Acknowledge your inner monologue, don't be ruled by it
- Expect to get 'spooked' occasionally and take action to reset your breathing
- Get your ideas into the arena early – nobody is expecting perfection
- Tune your internal dials, e.g. volume, pace and body language, to the external world
- Focus on the dialogue in the room, not the monologue in your head

A clear and supportive inner monologue is the first step towards unlocking your business voice. Make sure your receptors are turned on and tuned in before you hit the play button.

CHAPTER 2

What Happens On The Outside

A common objective of participants attending my workshops is, 'How do I build rapport with a roomful of strangers?'

Of course, attempting to connect with the individual personalities of a large audience would be an unmanageable strain. The good news is that we don't have to do this. The old maxim that we can't please all the people all of the time rings just as true with building rapport.

At the beginning of any piece of communication, the first thing other people look for, before the speaker even opens their mouth, is whether they're truly present. It's no more complex than that. However, it's all too easy to allow the distractions in our head to get in the way of our thread. The audience will often misinterpret this distraction and lose confidence in us and what we're trying to say. Whether we're addressing one person in a meeting, ten in a presentation, or even 1,000 at a conference, we first need to create rapport by sharing the moment and space equally with the recipients of our message.

While this may sound as if it should come naturally, it does demand some groundwork. Have you ever started to speak before you and the audience are ready? If you've never thought in those terms, look at it another way – how difficult is it to speak, collect your next thought and hold other people's attention all at the same time? If you've ever noticed you're losing your audience before you've even got going, then neither party was ready. It's easier to get them to your preferred destination if you both take off from the same place.

To back up this concept, I'm going to share three easy-to-digest lessons and give you an opportunity to test the theory for yourselves with some simple exercises.

Lesson #1 – Connection comes from being present

In terms of unlocking your business voice, start by focusing on being present and making a connection before you attempt to make your point.

Try this simple two-part exercise that demonstrates what it takes to be present.

PART ONE

Find a partner – a colleague, friend or family member.

Assign yourselves A and B. Count alternately from one to three continuously for approximately twenty seconds. A starts with one, B follows with two, A with three, and then B starts again with one, and so on.

Was that harder or easier than you thought it would be? Either way, you're ready for Part Two.

PART TWO

Replace the number 'Two' with a clap, so the only spoken numbers are now one and three. E.g. A says, 'One', B claps, A says, 'Three', B says, 'One', A claps, B says, 'Three', and so on for twenty seconds.

Hopefully, it all went wrong at some point.

A short sequence of three actions and only two of you performing them means it doesn't quite fit. In Part Two, the stakes are higher. You're likely planning the next move in your head now that it's a mixture of counting and clapping, and it doesn't work so well under pressure. No matter how hard you concentrate, it goes wrong, and that's when the magic happens. Did you both break into a smile or possibly laugh at the nonsense of it all when you went wrong? If you did, did you notice how your body language opened up? Maybe you and your partner subconsciously started to mirror each other. All of a sudden, you're out of your own head and present with the other person. Most importantly, you've made a connection with them.

Lesson outcome: by letting go of planning the moment, you can spontaneously ignite rapport and that's when the magic happens. Although it's great fun, repeating that exercise with the same person immediately after the first go isn't particularly useful, because rapport

37

building is unconscious and not something you can earn solely with your intellect.

Lesson #2 – The potential downside of playing it safe

In meetings, have you noticed that some people get a better reception than others, even when their message is controversial or unpopular? It would be all too easy to pin this on their job status, reputation or even company politics, all of which can leave you feeling pretty powerless.

What is definitely in your control, though, are the non-verbal signals you give off that people see and read before they hear and digest what you have to say. Have you ever considered that you might be rewarding or punishing others with your non-verbal communication? I thought that was an extreme statement when I first heard it, but the reality is that you can never turn off this element of your communication. You're always communicating something, even if you think you're playing it safe and not giving anything away.

I had a personal example of this a few years back while working for a training consultancy. One of my colleagues commented, 'Simon doesn't seem to like me nor respect my views.' That was the impression I had made on them.

Fortunately, another colleague, who had known me for longer, prevented any conflict developing by pointing out, 'That's just Simon's thinking face. It means you've actually said something he thought was worth processing.'

That's why I tell my clients to be careful what signals their listening face may be giving out, even when they think they're not giving anything away. Almost all of us unintentionally programme how people listen to us by how we listen to them. In my workshops, I illustrate this point with an exercise that achieves the same result over and over again, even after ten years of working with all types of people.

This is how it works.

I'll randomly pick a handful of participants and take them outside the room. Out of sight and earshot of everyone else, I'll brief them to enter the room, one at a time, and walk to the far end and back again. But here's the crucial instruction: they must do it as neutrally as possible. For the exercise to work, it's important that they're *neutral* not natural.

Obviously, there are different interpretations of the concept of neutrality. If, when I'm setting up the exercise, I'm pushed to expand on what I mean by this, I'll add something along the lines of, 'As if you're walking to another meeting room and not really taking in your surroundings'.

Meanwhile, my colleague inside the room is instructing the rest of the group to make a mental note of the effect each person entering the room has on them. After each of my group – let's call them the 'volunteers' – has left the room, my colleague records on a flip chart the words the observing group members use to describe the signals that person was giving off and the impression they made on them. It's important that this exercise can't be seen or heard by the others waiting outside the room to 'walk the walk'.

By the time all of my volunteers have completed their part of the task, the flip chart inside the room is full of words, although they're deliberately not assigned to any individual, and they are always scarily consistent. I thank the volunteers and ask them to reveal to the observing group the brief I gave them. Quite often, there's a bit of a gasp when my colleague then explains what was going on inside the room and exposes the contents of the flip chart.

Usually it's filled with words and phrases like:

- Disinterested
- In a hurry
- Preoccupied
- Distant
- Unconfident
- Bored

Sometimes there are more extreme examples, for instance 'annoyed' or 'angry'.

Of course, this is totally unfair, because the brief was for the volunteers to be as neutral as possible, not any of the above. Nobody intentionally chooses to have this effect on people they are trying to influence.

Lesson outcome: playing it safe with non-verbal communication is a false security, because dialling down your body language, contact and facial expressions too much is likely to be interpreted negatively by the recipient.

Lesson #3 – Hook the audience with your conclusion

Many books I've read on the subject of public speaking tend to focus on the *transmit* part of unlocking your business voice. That is only half the story. Great speakers, leaders and people of influence leave equal space for the *receive* part of their communication, too. In other words, what they can do to put others in the best place to listen to what they need to tell them.

The importance of this is backed up by what I'm often asked to improve or fix:

- Being clear
- Losing people in the detail
- Avoiding revisiting the same conversations

Paradoxically, the time and effort we put into preparing our content and shaping a sound and logical argument can work against us if we get too fixated with our side of the communication equation. How can this be? Surely our investment in knowing what we're talking about is what prevents us from looking foolish, and that is arguably the worst outcome for anyone in business.

Although it's always important to know what we're talking about, I would urge people to be careful with this assumption. It's tempting to believe that the better we know the content, the sharper we'll deliver it. The problem is that it's easy to become seduced by the quality of our argument and how it threads together, and in doing so, forget that

41

the person on the receiving end is hearing it for the first time. To be convinced by it, they need to arrive at the same insights we've spent the time to prepare and refine. This takes an investment of brain power on their part, and that's why we need to hook them early.

Hit them first with the conclusion and make allowances for their thought processes. Build that into your preparation and let go of needing to know every last detail of your subject. You'll know if you're not doing this if you end up talking faster and faster in an increasingly frustrating attempt to be understood.

To show how easy it is to remedy this, I'd like to share one of my favourite coaching assignments.

A few years ago, I was working with 'Jerry', a senior project manager with a multinational private sector organisation. Jerry dreaded the phrase 'Can you just give me the headlines?' and felt deflated every time he heard it. That was the last thing he wanted to do; he wanted to take listeners on the same journey he'd been on – working through the detail of the situation; defining the problem; researching and benchmarking against similar projects. Only then would he be able to share the possible solutions and their impacts on the business.

Jerry's frustration was that he'd done his due diligence, preparing what he needed to say (so he wasn't making it up as he went along), and because it was now crystal clear in his head, he could deliver it very quickly to senior stakeholders. Knowing they were busy people, he felt sure that this was the right approach.

Therein lies the problem. People are much more interested in outcomes than in processes. Many of us were told at school that we needed to show our 'workings' – how we had arrived at our findings, what our assumptions were, where we found out that piece of information, etc. But in the world of fast-paced business, that's a lesson worth unlearning when we need to hook our audience quickly and make our message more receivable.

Jerry was admired internally as a bit of a miracle worker, often delivering complex projects ahead of time. However, his preference for explaining situations in great detail was wearing a bit thin with some of the Senior Leadership Team. The business was in an accelerated period of growth through acquisition and there was less time to make decisions, while more attention was being given to anyone worth listening to. Unfortunately for Jerry, nobody was paying much attention to what he had to say.

Happily, I was able to direct Jerry to a satisfactory ending. I shared with him my Hourglass Principle of Communication which explains the relationship between how to build your argument versus how others need to receive it. It's a simple visual tool for ensuring you get the most benefit from your preparation work, making you easier to understand and consequently propelling your powers of influence into warp drive.

Here's how it works in a nutshell. Picture in your mind an ancient wooden-framed hourglass. As you turn the hourglass over, the sand flows smoothly from the top bulb into the bottom, and as the top bulb gradually empties, the rate of flow steadily increases until the last grains

43

arrive with a flourish at the crest of the pile below. The bottom bulb is now full and primed.

That is how you build the content of what you want to say – one grain at a time, until you arrive at your conclusion, which is represented by the last grains sitting at the top of the pile.

To unlock your business voice and start the communication flow, turn the hourglass once more. When you do, the first grains of sand to pass through the constriction into the empty and receptive chamber below are the last ones that arrived when you were formulating the content. In other words, start by disclosing your results and conclusions.

That's the way people usually feel most comfortable receiving information, so it buys you their precious listening time.

Lesson outcome: if you've ever been unfairly accused of waffling and not getting to the point, here's your remedy. Flip from transmit to receive mode to get your message across and gain commitment for action from others. This is easier and far less frustrating than trying to speed your way through the entirety of what you want to say. Remember the hourglass metaphor, and that it is perfectly OK for your audience to flip the hourglass back. It's a great sign of their engagement.

In the vast majority of situations, your audience is not judging you. Other people do, however, expect you to equal the investment they make in listening to you by working to establish a connection with them before you speak. To label this as 'small talk' is unhelpful; rather, it's a critical precursor to unlocking your business voice, and involves turning on the rest of your senses.

Remember:

- Take a breath
- Open up your frame to welcome people
- Make authentic eye contact and dare to smile
- Turn your dial up a notch when required
- Above all, be authentic

Your audience's inner monologue is making a real-time judgement on how much airtime you're worth, and you won't get any credits for burdening them with the strain of reaching your conclusions, so throw them your best hook early. If the connection is strong from the outset, you'll earn the opportunity to prove your thinking.

Why bother changing?

Have you ever thought that if you don't get noticed, you won't get preyed upon? That's perfectly natural. It's a survival tactic that is hardcoded into the human brain.

The problem with this tactic, however, is that it means staying where you are and stagnating. If moving forward in your career is your goal, it will be much more dependent on the impact you have on those around you (both within your organisation and externally) than on acquiring more technical knowledge and expertise. Do you think you have the right skills or tools to achieve that impact?

Don't panic – you've earned the right to make it happen. Nobody is incapable of making this transition.

I consistently hear participants in my workshops tell me how they've benefitted from working with the VOICE Methodology in the following ways:

- 💬 They are better at dealing with nerves
- 💬 They have enhanced self-esteem and confidence

- They have deeper commitment from colleagues
- They are comfortable managing healthy conflict
- They feel valued as an expert worth listening to

What would each of these benefits mean for you? Take a moment and make them personal, because what you're about to embark on will have a cost so you need to be convinced that the juice is worth the squeeze. The thousands of people I've worked with assure me it is.

If you want to hear what some of these people have said about my methodology and what they have gained from putting it into practice, please check out our Success Stories at www.myfirsttrainers.com

Avoiding some common mistakes

In the spirit of prevention being better than cure, I want to expose the mistakes I've seen people make while attempting to improve their communication skills. Before you work on anything else, being aware of these mistakes will save you time and wasted effort.

In no particular order:

- Trying to process unhelpful generic advice, e.g. 'You need more gravitas'
- Attempting to emulate the most engaging speakers on TED talks
- Loading up on content and hoping it will do the work for them

- Misinterpreting what the audience needs
- Not practising in a safe environment and discovering what doesn't work

I've certainly made some of these mistakes throughout my career. So before we dive into the work, here are a few words of sanity to avoid you making them in future.

It's tempting to take other people's well-meant advice, but it tends to reflect what's worked for them in the past, and there's no guarantee that it'll work for you. Also, there's not much value in hearing what you need to have more or less of, for example gravitas, energy, charisma and so forth, if the advice is not followed up with how to get it. It's no good telling a drowning person what the water looks like and not throwing them a lifebelt.

TED talks are, of course, truly inspirational and well worth watching, especially if you want to learn how accomplished speakers hook their audience and often disrupt their thinking. However, have you noticed that all great speakers have a clear sense of who they are? Their different styles of delivery come with their different personalities. That is why it's crucial to understand and accept how others naturally see you in the business arena – your business casting – rather than trying to stick on other people's tricks. Otherwise you'll confuse yourself and everyone else. Be comfortable as your best authentic self and make it work for you.

By way of illustration, here's what happened when I first met the UK Managing Director of a multinational technology company. The conversation went a bit like this:

'Simon, can you make me funny? I hate following the sales team on stage at conferences as they always get the crowd on their feet.'

I'm glad I had the nerve to ask the obvious question on our first meeting.

'Are you funny?'

'No, not really,' came the instant reply.

'OK, so what are you? When it's all working, how do you think you come across?'

He thought for a while, and then I saw on his face the instant the answer came to him.

'I've been told I'm like the favourite science teacher at school. I can explain complex ideas in a relatively simple and fun way.'

I took the opportunity to land this insight, which after all had come from him and not me.

'Brilliant, let's use that as your natural casting and add some skills and techniques to make it work for you, even when you don't feel at your best.'

49

From this point on, the work we did together had a firm foundation and the MD was more comfortable in his own style and confident in the skills he'd acquired to get his point across.

Unlocking your business voice is the logical and appropriate next stage in your career development. It's now time to make sure you leverage the knowledge and wisdom you have acquired. The methodology I've designed for you will give you the framework to achieve this and get results fast.

CHAPTER 3

Put The Prize Before The Process

Let me start this chapter with an admission. I work in Corporate Training as a communication skills coach and workshop facilitator. I once asked my son, a surly teenager at the time, what he told his mates at school when they asked him what his dad did. His reply was typically to the point.

'I just ask them if they know the film *The King's Speech*. If they do, I say that's what my dad does, only for business people.'

I've found myself using this as an ice-breaker at networking events. Of course, it only works when people have seen the film, but nevertheless it is pretty fit for purpose.

However, my admission is not really about what I do. It has much more to do with the effectiveness of training and the responsibility I have to help the people I work with. My overriding concern is that the industry

53

I've come to love working in can be guilty of delivering what I call 'air-freshener training'.

My definition of air-freshener training is when everybody has a lovely time on the day because all the theories and models make perfect sense and 'smell nice'. The problem with this type of training is the risk that the benefit will only be temporary, and I'm not alone in this fear. It is shared by many excellent training facilitators out there. The effect of the training seems to wear off only a few steps outside of wherever it was delivered. That's why people are asked to fill in the 'happy sheets', aka feedback forms, before they leave the room.

If you fancy a giggle, check out my *Training Crimes* series, made in partnership with DPG (Developing People Globally), via the YouTube channel link at MyFirstTrainers.com.

The solution requires you and me to work together from this point onwards. That means you being specific about your objectives and the outcomes you want to achieve. My part of the contract will be to share tips and techniques and examples of how the My Business Voice Methodology® has helped others.

Let's get going on a 'DIWY' – do it with you – basis and throw away that can of air freshener.

Make it personal – set your goals

Think through, evaluate and commit to the outcomes you will need to make this work worthwhile. I'm going to help you to do this, so you won't be left hanging with a plausible supposition and a blank piece of paper. But before I do this, let me share a couple of reasons why this is such an important first step.

Many people start with the mindset, 'I'm usually fine with people, but there's one stakeholder I just can't get onside.' They do the same things, over and over again, getting the same results. I hear this frequently during workshops and coaching sessions, and it seems to be consistent across many industry sectors, cultures and demographics.

What I teach works much better if people put themselves at the centre of the solution and reframe the goal: 'I want to be better at working out what stakeholders want and to what degree I can help them.' This now puts them much more in control of unlocking their business voice as they can work on reverse engineering from that future outcome.

There will always be individuals who are hard for you to communicate with. However, if you make yourself the focus of the goal, it's much more personal and rewarding.

Another common mistake people make is trying to work on everything at once. Instead, they need to say to themselves, 'I'm already a great communicator. This is the next thing I want to work on.'

It'll become overwhelming if you try and change your communication style too drastically, as well as changing your personality while you're at it. The key to reaping the return on your investment is making the juice worth the squeeze. Buy into the benefits of the My Business Voice Methodology® and make it your own, unlocking your business voice. Choose and commit to one specific future outcome at a time and apply the methodology to that. You can always repeat the prescription.

The big four diagnostic questions

I have a good friend who works as a senior project manager in the IT industry, managing seven- and eight-figure budgets. He and I follow the same football club and often chat about his work on the way to games. I love his blunt and brutal insights into his world, which he puts down to his Scottish roots.

On one notable occasion, he nearly made me choke on my pre-match beer with his sardonic declaration, 'Ya see, the problem is, Simon, I've got a bunch of Business Analysts that willnae talk to anyone.'

Although this was probably a slight exaggeration, his point was well made in the context of attempting to analyse a business function via email exchanges without talking to the people who ran it. I truly believe that the most damaging conversations in business are the ones that don't happen rather than the ones that do.

My advice to my clients is always to seek out opportunities to speak with colleagues. It not only raises your profile, but it also builds relationships, sharing information and ideas. The trick is to make your communication count.

I have designed four questions to help you focus and get up close and personal with your goals. In thinking about your responses, you will increase your self-awareness and squeeze out and purify the juice from the My Business Voice Methodology®.

- When are you at your most influential at work?
- Which situations most commonly lead to deadlock?
- What happens if you're thrown in at the deep end?
- Who do you know who always makes an impact?

At this point, you may find some questions clearer and easier to answer than others. It doesn't matter. I'll add more context to each one throughout the rest of this chapter.

In the diagnostic exercises below, feel free to skip ahead to the question(s) that resonated with you most strongly on the first reading. However, I would highly recommend you revisit all of them before moving on as you'll get a deeper diagnosis and a clearer idea of what you need to work on as we get into more detail throughout the book. I promise you this isn't navel gazing without a purpose.

Diagnostic exercise #1 – when are you at your most influential at work?

There's a risk that you'll now be agonising over finding the most critical situation where your audience was hanging on to your every word and you were able to drive through a mega-strategic initiative. If you've got an example of when this happened, that's fantastic, but if not, let me illustrate what I mean by influential.

Two men were on a train with an out-of-order toilet – OK, hardly the stuff of Elon Musk (Tesla) or Jeff Bezos (Amazon). I was travelling south after a busy day of lectures in London on a rush hour stopping service and, as usual, it was standing room only. I noticed a man sitting in the single occupancy seat just outside the toilet with a glass of wine in one hand and a seriously thick book in the other.

What a marvellous idea, I thought. 'Bookman' was clearly content in his private space and intended to stay there all the way to the south coast.

All was well, and the carriage gradually emptied as we passed through suburbia until eventually we arrived at East Croydon. This was where the 'Hero' of our little story joined our carriage and immediately headed for the toilet, only to find that it was out of order.

He studied the small square sign to the left of the door then dialled the customer service number. Although I could only hear his side of the conversation, it was clear that Hero was being passed from department to department. What struck me as impressive was the clarity of his mission and his assertive, not aggressive, tone.

When he eventually spoke to someone who was willing to engage, he calmly made the point that the sign invited passengers to report faults with the facility and promised a remedial response. His insistence was that they honour that commitment and tell him what would happen as a result of his call.

Hero patiently listened to whatever was being said on the other end of the line and then repeated his original point, skilfully avoiding the temptation to sound more and more frustrated, which I'm pretty sure he was feeling. What happened next illustrates the difference between influence and persuasion, something that often comes up in discussions with the leadership teams I work with.

Remember Bookman was sitting, engrossed in his book and glass of wine, next to the toilet. His peace had been broken and unintentionally he'd been drawn into the discussion. Even though Hero hadn't been raising his voice, his proximity meant that he was hard to ignore, and Bookman wasn't happy.

Bookman's first attempt at regaining his peace and quiet was typically British: a fleeting and disapproving eye movement accompanied by an under-the-breath tut. Hero chose to take the bait and politely but equally assertively explained why he was making the call and that it would end when he had got the answer the sign promised. Bookman now didn't have anywhere to go; he couldn't argue with Hero's logic or the manner in which it was delivered, so he offered a placating smile and attempted to reconnect with his book. But of course, he couldn't; he was now involved, as was I.

Then came the pivotal moment in our story. As Hero returned to his call, Bookman intervened again, only this time with some advice.

'Tell them it happens way too often. We pay too much already for a second-rate service.'

Hero's reply was again polite and assertive.

'If you have your own point to make, may I suggest you call the number yourself?'

That's exactly what Bookman did. He put down his book, took out his phone, got up, walked to the sign and dialled the number. My stop came just as he got through and started more or less the same conversation as Hero had had five minutes earlier. For a moment before I left the train, I could hear two conversations about the same thing, side by side, yet totally independent of each other.

What is the key point to the story? Have you worked it out?

It's all about your power to influence others indirectly and sometimes unintentionally rather than using deliberate tactics and techniques to persuade them. You could argue that Hero 'suggested' that Bookman make the call, but that would be missing the point. That clearly wasn't Hero's intention or goal. It happened because Bookman was influenced by Hero's clarity and resolve and the effect Hero's communication style had on him.

I thought long and hard about including my 'toilet on a train' story, worrying that it may not have the gravitas people would expect from a serious business book. But for me, it illustrates the point perfectly. You may not immediately be aware when your business voice is unlocked and working to influence others, because it happens naturally and effortlessly.

Your answer to this question will contribute to the *Vocation* and *Casting* parts of the My Business Voice Methodology®. The possessive adjective 'my' implies that you'll end up with a methodology that you own which works for you. Like all bad medicine, generic formulas will just go straight through you, no matter how hard you swallow, and therefore have no long-term benefits.

> **Exercise.** Think about when other people have moved in your direction without you pushing them to do so. It's much easier to spot the result rather than the process. For example, you may have noticed a colleague quoting you during meetings or adopting a similar style of reporting or presenting. Make a few notes on what actually happened in the style of the police recording an incident; you want evidence rather than analysis at this stage.

Diagnostic exercise #2 – which situations most commonly lead to deadlock?

Being stuck in deadlock is the antithesis to being influential. In reality, it probably hasn't happened that often in your career, but it's so frustrating that it can stick out as being more memorable than it should be.

What will be interesting and helpful to you is identifying the antecedents to reaching deadlock. There will likely be some trends and patterns that emerge. Commonly they include:

- Types of people with whom you just don't 'gel'
- Time pressure, even though this can sometimes help
- One side abusing their status and the other being entrenched in 'being right'
- Conflicting agendas and no unifying sense of purpose
- No one cares enough about finding a workaround solution

Do any of these sound familiar? They're certainly the main causes of deadlock I hear from my clients, particularly from business partners working with stakeholders in technical environments.

The last bullet point is the killer. Instead of working to find a solution, many people end up walking away. Don't dismiss this as a legitimate strategy, provided it's a deliberate one.

I would urge you to look up the work of Ken Thomas and Ralph Kilmann on conflict management. Their TKI™ instrument is based on forty years of observation and robust scientific research. In essence, the message is to pick your battles *before* going to war. Invest in the ones that are worth winning, choose your tactics depending on the importance of maintaining a relationship with the opposition, and walk away from those where there is nothing to be gained. At least then you'll live to fight another day.

The universal starting point for tackling deadlock is to try something different, hence the *Experiment* part of the VOICE model. Of course, this requires time, effort and perseverance, because you're unlikely to get it right first time. That's exactly why you need to have a range of things you can try, because whatever or whoever is in your way is not going to help you by declaring the cause of the deadlock. Life would be so much easier if they did.

Imagine a difficult colleague announcing, 'I think the reason we're not getting anywhere is that I'm playing the status card to knock down your insights, dangling the time pressure sword over your head, and had made up my mind that we wouldn't get on when I reluctantly agreed to this meeting.'

The big irony is that other people think you don't know or notice what they're up to because they don't come out and declare it. This is utter nonsense, and academic research has rather tidily labelled it and other mental shortcuts as Cognitive Social Bias.

Two of my favourites are at play here:

- 💬 The illusion of asymmetric insight
- 💬 The illusion of transparency

Asymmetric insights fool people into thinking that they can read others, but others can't read them. Transparency overestimates people's view of how well others know them and underestimates their ability to read others. My important message here is to trust your instincts. Diagnose what's going on from the other person's perspective and commit to changing your communication style first in an attempt to break the deadlock. At this point, I'm only asking you to take the first step and diagnose. I'll look at different tactics you can try in the next section.

> **Exercise.** Analyse the situations at work that have led to deadlock with colleagues and see if you can identify patterns in the causes. It's important to resist the temptation to make any judgements when you do this, about either yourself or the other side. Make a note of what you usually do and how other people have reacted to what you've tried in the past to break the deadlock.

Diagnostic exercise #3 – what happens if you're thrown in at the deep end?

Have you heard of the Cassandra metaphor? The term originates in Greek mythology. Cassandra was the daughter of King Priam and Queen Hecuba of Troy. Apollo, the god of the sun and music, gave Cassandra the power of prophecy in an effort to seduce her. Cassandra spurned his advances, and Apollo put a curse on her in a fit of rage. Her gift became an anathema; despite their accuracy and importance, her warnings would never be heeded by anyone she spoke to.

Do you ever find yourself feeling a bit like this? It's uncomfortable and frustrating; you know everything you need to know about an issue and yet can't get others to take notice. There's no disputing your depth of knowledge or expertise, but ask yourself whether your *intention* is always as clear. This is the additional feature your content needs to get heard and that's why it's in the VOICE model.

Your intention is a choice you make first in the mind. It is then carried in the language you use, the simpler the better, and finally delivered through your physical state and vocal quality. Mind, body and voice: your fully integrated hard drive.

The following examples are of two highly competent people I've worked with from contrasting industries, both of whom found themselves in unfamiliar territory, but for different reasons.

'Alex' works for a Biotechnology heavy hitter. Her specialism is the algorithms that make sense of raw data. Our discussions centred on a global industry conference which she'd been invited to attend by her commercial team.

Alex's work is all about understanding the context behind the numbers, the degree of flexibility in accuracy and the physical constraints of what's possible. Her job at the conference was to present the 'proof of concept' of a new cloud-based solution. Alex's dilemma was how to deliver the impact her commercial team wanted while safeguarding the company's reputation for 'good science'. Given the likely pace of the conversations at the conference, there wouldn't be time to qualify and explore the significance of the results from the pilot in the same way her written report had done.

Although she had a professional duty to be impartial, there was also a commercial need for her not to look over cautious and slow. My solution was that she needed to simplify her language, be more confident in explaining the consequences of her findings and focus on what the audience would care about. It worked. Alex was able to engage and excite everyone she spoke to at the conference while safeguarding her professional integrity.

Here's another instance of being thrown in at the deep end, albeit this time where the issue was more about appearing to be the authority without the knowledge to back up this status.

'Barry' works in financial services as a systems engineer. Barry's nightmare scenario is when his boss asks him to step in and represent him at Senior Leadership Team meetings, often with little time to prepare. He told me this sends him into a panic – what if he gets asked a technical question about a project he's only had limited exposure to?

I reassured Barry that what his boss needed him to do was to champion the importance of the projects the team was working on rather than be the expert on the detail behind them. I coached him to elevate his thinking to a more strategic level and therefore influence decisions in the same way his boss would have done if he'd been there. To do this, Barry had to let go of the need to explain, clarify and justify, which were his default intentions and why he believed he had the status of expert in the first place.

All credit to Barry – he realised that to move from being an expert to being a thought leader, a more appropriate casting at the Senior Leadership

Team meetings, he needed to be more probing, challenging and convincing. I knew he'd made it when he told me he'd been asked a question about a project he wasn't too familiar with, and he responded by saying, 'I don't know, but I can always find out. What's the question behind that question?'

In other words, Barry was probing the intention, not the detail. He told me how empowering that felt for him.

These two examples represent different ends of the same problem: when being the technical expert isn't the role the situation and/or the company requires. In Alex's case, she had too much knowledge and not enough interest from the audience in the detail. Conversely, Barry would have had too little information to fulfil his role at the Senior Leadership meeting if his only job had been to update. What they had in common was the solution.

Put your content aside and focus on how you need to affect your audience. Your job whenever you communicate is to choose the most appropriate *intentions* to drive your content and get the result you require.

> **Exercise.** Reflect for a while on the situations where you've felt uncharacteristically out of your depth and think about what made you feel like that. This requires some potentially difficult self-analysis, so do it in private and on a day when you're feeling upbeat about yourself. My challenge for you is to see if you can uncover the underlying cause behind the obvious symptom.

Diagnostic exercise #4 – who do you know who always makes an impact?

Although I've had the privilege to know many such individuals over my years in business, the person who most immediately springs to mind is my boss at American Express. He is not an extrovert, nor would he describe himself as particularly charismatic. He doesn't have a velvety voice that people could listen to for hours on end. Yet he has certainly unlocked his business voice and others respect what he has to say, even when they vehemently disagree with him, which is rare.

I particularly like the way he makes people feel that he's heard them, which is not necessarily the same thing as listening to them. He's mastered the power of the pause and usually talks in short, measured sentences, so that his tone maintains its quiet intensity from the first syllable to the last.

Like many great leaders, he is generous in sharing his knowledge and experience. I've learnt from our many conversations over the years that it's taken a while for him to refine and perfect his communication style. He told me that he's assimilated aspects from the great communicators he's encountered in his career and blended them into what works for him. That's the key to his success: observing everything and then figuring out and remaining true to what works for him. For each characteristic he's adopted, he's rejected many more that, although great to admire in others, wouldn't come across as natural if he tried to claim them as his own.

Of course, nowadays we're not restricted to learning from the people we know or have met. YouTube and in particular TED talks offer us a prodigious array of subjects and speakers to devour. Therein can lie the problem, because just about every speaker we see has something to offer.

It can be easy to get bogged down and spend a whole lot of time trying to distil all the awesome techniques on show. Instead of unlocking your business voice, you may get trapped in a never-ending quest for perfection. To this point, you're better off working on the prevention rather than attempting to find the cure when you're confused and overwhelmed. Subtly change the focal point of the lens through which you *observe* from how the person is speaking to how the audience is listening. This is far more straightforward to interpret, because the audience takes a pretty consistent journey to buy into the speaker's message.

If you haven't seen them in action already, take a moment to look up Sir Ken Robinson, Brené Brown and Dan Pink on TED.com. You'll find them easily as they are among the most popular TED talks of all time. Notice that they've got their own distinctive approach. I was particularly conscious of the differences in pitch, pace and body language the first time I saw them. Look again, and spot how the audience is responding. This time, you'll become more aware of the similarities than the differences.

Now turn this to your advantage and combine the *Observation* and *Casting* elements of the My Business Voice Methodology® to explore the best way for you to take the audience on the same journey, using the content at your disposal and the most appropriate, for you, style of delivery.

Exercise. Make a list of your top five role models for unlocking your business voice whom you have worked with directly or have met more than a handful of times. Repeat this for people you only know through the media. It doesn't matter which sector or discipline they represent; the more varied, the better. You now have a top ten list of highly skilled communicators that's personal to you.

Now I need you to reduce this list down to your top three based on how they affect their audience. Make a note of what they do rather than how they do it, and take this forward as your goal.

Whatever thoughts you've had during this chapter, let me assure you that it's been a good use of your internal processing unit. This is the data you'll need to unlock your business voice. Forgive the technology analogy – of course, this type of work is very much a part of being human and not a machine. The challenge lies in the simple truth that you can already communicate; it's something you do every day. This work can appear ambiguous, and in the past was commonly given the classification of 'soft skills'. I personally dislike this label because it detracts from the very 'hard' and important outcomes that I've seen achieved.

Equally, I'd understand if you were apprehensive about this work on the grounds that it would make you come across as fake and inauthentic. In one of my first workshops, an MBA (Master of Business Administration) student put me firmly in my place when I announced to the group that I was an actor.

'I'm not here to learn how to be an actor. I want to know about being more confident when I have to speak up in difficult situations.'

They were absolutely right. The world doesn't need any more unemployed actors. What it does need are more unlocked and empowered business voices. I had positioned the workshop in entirely the wrong way, and I was grateful to learn this lesson early on in my coaching career.

A great antidote to the fear of being inauthentic would be to watch 'The Importance Of Being Inauthentic': Mark Bowden at TEDxToronto. I really like Mark's style, and he's clearly an authority on body language and how to influence your audience. What I take from his central message is that being inauthentic in the right way, at the right time and when appropriate to your audience, adds to your power to influence them. Rather than worrying about being inauthentic as you develop new skills and techniques, make sincerity the goal in everything you do and say, and all will be OK.

The initiation and planning phases are now complete. Now it's time for execution.

PART 2

The Five Step Process To Unlocking Your Business Voice

CHAPTER 4

How The My Business Voice Methodology® Works For You

I will now guide you through the My Business Voice Methodology® that will ultimately unlock your business voice and carry you forward in your career.

There are five steps to the VOICE model:

- Vocation
- Observation
- Intention
- Casting
- Experiment

Over the next few chapters, I will explain each step in detail and offer you powerful hints and tips to help you to apply them. These steps are all important, because together they will ensure that you get long-term results. However, they are not mutually exclusive, nor do they need to be implemented in strict order. I recommend that you absorb the whole model in one sitting, then make a decision on what you want to work on first, and focus and commit to making that come to life.

As you see that small changes really do make a big difference, the likelihood is you'll want to come back and look at other ways to make similar breakthroughs. My advice is to think of the five steps more in terms of the combinations they offer to unlock your business voice, rather than searching for a single potentially elusive key. Otherwise, you may be searching for a long time with little or no result, and your business voice will remain locked away.

Allow me to introduce you to one of my all-time communication heroes, Stephen Covey (whose surname is, appropriately, almost an anagram of 'voice'), an author and, above all else, an outstanding educator.

He's arguably best known for his book *The 7 Habits of Highly Effective People*®, but there are many more books and articles of his to gorge upon. I highly recommend you take the opportunity to read at least one of his books and benefit from his refreshingly blunt insight and wisdom. His observations are extremely relevant to the relentless pace of business today.

By way of encouragement, watch an online interview with Stephen Covey on Success Television, recorded in 2008, called 'On Choosing Success' http://site.successtelevision.biz/leadershipskills/index.php/uncategorized/stephen-covey-video-on-change-management/. During the interview, he offers the perfect context for commencing our work on The Voice Methodology®: 'Beware of being a captive of your past and instead own the space between stimulus and response and exploit your freedom to choose.' Covey clearly states that you don't need to be at the mercy of nature or nurture.

Make unlocking your business voice your product of choice. It doesn't matter who or where you are in your career progression, if your business voice remains locked away, this will most certainly be an impediment to achieving your future success.

Students are amongst my favourite people to work with because they are often challenging, but in a highly constructive way. They're not into bluff or waffle and they see through these very quickly. If you get them onside early enough in the process, they'll add their own insights and embed the learning with you.

One such student encounter I had during an Executive Presence workshop is an excellent example of what you will gain from being more aware of your communication style, even before you do anything to change it.

I had just seen a colleague, David, get off on the wrong foot with a group of highly introverted and reflective financial consultants on a two-day offsite convention on Influencing and Persuading. He had opened the first session enthusiastically, focusing on the fun element we had planned for them later in the day when a magician would bring to life the less obvious facets of how people are influenced by performing some of his tricks. However, the audience sat there in silence and didn't react to any of David's prompts.

After only a couple of minutes, David made a brave decision and changed direction. He sat down, picked up the workbook and clicked on the first PowerPoint slide which detailed the objectives and agenda for the two days. He also slowed down and moderated his voice, both in terms of volume and tone. His next few sentences were shorter and packed with facts.

Immediately, I could feel the participants in the room relax and connect with him. The big irony to this story is that the most talked about session over the two days, the one which the participants had enjoyed the most, was the one with the magician. David had been right all along, the audience just didn't know it.

I really applaud the courage David showed in that moment of mini crisis to resist the temptation to go into 'comfort zone overdrive' by using his extrovert style to demand the participants' attention. What worked so well was dialling down the extremities of what came naturally to him, so that he could bridge the communication gap and get them on board.

That's the big encouragement and why, with David's permission, I share this story with my students. There is no need to get bogged down analysing something you do anyway and every day. The fact is, you are well ahead of most people by being more aware of what's going on around you, so if things seem to be going wrong, just stop and try something else instead.

CHAPTER 5

Step 1: Vocation

Human multi-media wonder

I'm reassured to see the growing movement on social media to re-humanise business, and this trend is flowing through the marketing campaigns of large companies. I'm also acutely aware of the rate of technological advancement and the impact that is having on the way business is conducted.

Gordon Moore, founder of Intel, wrote an essay in 1965 in which he predicted how computer chips would double in power every two years. His prediction proved to be accurate for the next fifty years and became 'Moore's Law'. It's reported that 40% of global productivity growth for the last two decades can be attributed to the expansion of technology made possible by chip performance and price.

Of course, there is a limit to how small a transistor can get, and that is why technology commentators have announced the demise of Moore's Law. Far from being bad news and heralding a slowdown in the global economy, it's regarded as a massively exciting opportunity to get creative and think 'Moore' about what we want from technology.

Pardon the pun; it was deliberate, because the new phrase people are using to describe this point of inflection in the application of technology is 'More than Moore'. This fundamental change in the way businesses need to grow, through innovation and creativity, has an immense impact on how people will need to communicate. To be successful, companies will need unlocked business voices that are both compelling and willing to share ideas, but understand the need to listen to others. A direct impact of the growth in the gig economy and continuing trend for employing contingency workers is that we'll need to hit the ground running and build rapport with colleagues faster.

As I'm suggesting with the subtitle 'Human multi-media wonder', you're already well equipped for this challenge. Your ability to react to something you've heard or to generate an idea and then express it is truly incredible. Computers are still a long way from emulating you.

However, one problem you may have that computers don't is getting in your own way. This has the reverse effect to what you identified by answering my first diagnostic question: 'When are you at your most influential at work?' Nobody is influenced by somebody who's struggling to convince themselves. My follow-up question is therefore, 'Are you setting the bar too high by trying to convince others every time you speak?'

Think on this for a moment and allow me to join the dots of what's been covered already:

- There are occasions when you're highly influential
- It's your *Vocation* to speak up, care about what you say and share ideas
- The lack of communication in business causes serious problems

At the risk of being controversial, I'm suggesting that the ability to persuade others is overrated in today's world of work. This might contradict everything you've been told, especially if you've ever attended a training course on 'How to Persuade Others' or read books with similar titles. My point has nothing to do with the legitimacy of being able to convince your colleagues, yet has plenty to do with not making that your sole aim or preoccupation.

If everything else you're doing is right and your content is robust, then you stand a pretty good chance of convincing other people, without even noticing that you're trying. I often demonstrate this idea by asking the group I'm working with for a show of hands in agreement if they enjoy buying things, and usually the majority of hands go up. I then ask whoever has raised their arm to keep it there if they enjoy being sold to. Now most of the hands are lowered, because the gratification associated with making our own mind up to buy something is entirely different to the resistance we subconsciously generate when somebody tries to sell us something.

The same is true for influencing and convincing. Most of us are open to being influenced, provided that the final decision is ours and not reliant on us being convinced by others, particularly if there is even the slightest hint of manipulation. This means that you can safely lower the bar and stop worrying whether you're convincing your audience when you speak.

Instead, remember to:

- Concentrate on knowing what's useful for them to get from you
- Make it your job to be easy to listen to
- Be present with them as they react to what you're telling them

Work through the following example, which is based on a real-life client case study. After reading this, apply the same methodology to your own scenario and make it real life and real time for you.

The problem. You are a Procurement Specialist in a large electrical manufacturer, working in a centralised function with the responsibility to collaborate with Senior Business Line Managers on a project by project basis. Last month, you advised on the appointment of an

85

external marketing agency needed to create the campaign to support an important new product innovation. This work included sitting on a shortlist selection panel with the Marketing Director responsible for the product launch.

Subsequent to you making your recommendation based on a robust scoring system, you have heard that the Marketing Director has gone with his gut and decided to appoint another agency based on its great ideas. This agency has no track record in your industry and may lack resources to manage a campaign of this size.

The solution. You schedule a meeting with the Marketing Director to discuss their decision. First decide why it's important to unlock your business voice and the benefits of doing so, and then think about the most effective way of doing so. Remember to let go of the burden of needing to convince all of the people all of the time; it will happen naturally if you just get out of your own way.

Write yourself a brief job description for your role in this conversation.

- What do you want to achieve as a realistic outcome?
- What are you going to do to fully understand the Marketing Director's position?
- How will you leverage your procurement expertise?

Hint – you won't get very far by telling them they've made the wrong decision.

The first part of the My Business Voice Methodology®, Vocation, is all about choosing your mindset and therefore your role in any piece of communication that you deliver. This will, and indeed should, vary depending on the situation, but absolutely not according to the personalities involved.

CHAPTER 6

Step 2: Observation

Beware Bandura's Bobo

There's nothing new about the concept of learning through observation. However, I want to start this chapter with a warning from history, courtesy of Albert Bandura's social learning study from the early 1960s. Bandura investigated the acquisition of social behaviours through observation and imitation. The study tested thirty-six girls and thirty-six boys, aged between three and six years old, specifically on their levels of aggression towards a toy doll named Bobo.

The boys and girls were divided into three equal test groups. The first group observed a male or female adult behaving aggressively towards Bobo. The second group observed an adult playing quietly and ignoring Bobo. The final group was the control and was not exposed to any 'modelling' behaviour.

Unsurprising, when the children were taken into the room containing Bobo, and a collection of other aggressive and non-aggressive toys, the first group behaved more aggressively towards the doll, imitating what they had observed. I am in danger of over-simplifying both the experiment and the results, and would therefore urge you to look up the study if you're interested in knowing more https://www.youtube.com/watch?v=dmBqwWUg8U.

The reason I've used Bandura's early work to introduce this chapter (despite the criticism he's had from psychologists and scientists) is because it demonstrates the human trait of imitating what we observe. I'm going to take this one step further and suggest that this is a passive response – it occurs subconsciously.

Of course, unlike my somewhat alarmist subtitle leading with 'Beware', this needn't be a cause for concern. Most of the time, we imitate the behaviours we observe that are useful and help us to communicate in the way we want to. However, on some occasions we probably 'catch' not so helpful behaviours from others. The core of the *Observation* part of the My Business Voice Methodology® is to take control of our imitation and make it a conscious and active step in unlocking our business voice.

To help you to do this, I'd like to share my experience of writing this book. After I made the commitment to get down and actually do it (the hardest decision I've made for quite a while), I noticed a shift in my behaviour. Although I have always regarded myself as pretty observant, I now endeavoured to record anything I thought would be useful. I wasn't selective about when this might happen, be it in a workshop, during a coaching session or even while watching trashy television. The trick was to do it little and often, and I disciplined myself not to overthink what I was recording at the time. I found the voice memo app on my smartphone brilliantly helpful for doing this, and these days it's nearly always with me so I can record my stream of consciousness at any time without much effort.

It's often the things that are easy to do that don't happen. Great intentions without a plan remain just that. Start recording useful and effective moments of communication, whenever and with whomever you see them, and apply this to unlocking your business voice. If you have a gut reaction to something, then it's worth recording. On this occasion, more is better, as you can filter the results afterwards.

Here's your plan.

Set a realistic time period. My suggestion is to look at your schedule and pick a period that includes meetings with a variety of internal and external contacts. Select a relatively short time limit on your first observation period; you're not trying to establish a permanent practice.

Make a contract with yourself. Develop a way of working that's practical to your work and lifestyle. I added five minutes of voice-recording my thoughts to my coming down ritual after workshops, coaching sessions and meetings.

Shout out to friends and colleagues. Ask them to share links to their favourite speakers. Make a point of asking someone you hold in high regard, but who has a significantly different style of working to yours.

You'll get better results by normalising this process, which you can do by simply sharing what you're doing with trusted friends and colleagues. What I'm asking you to do is to collect evidence to back up what your instincts are probably telling you already, and then distil these observations into a plan of action. You may need some guidance on creating your plan, so here is a case study to help you.

'Sophia' works as an Asset Manager with responsibility for a property portfolio. We met a few years back, and I agreed to review her *Observation* analysis and plan at the end of the month, giving her a few weeks to complete the task.

The colleague she had noticed most frequently was her Head of Research, 'Alistair'. She was particularly impressed by his ability to hold his ground when challenged during external briefings to the investment community. She noticed how 'Alistair' often smiled in acknowledgement when asked a particularly probing question and managed to come across as respectful, even when completely disagreeing with the point being made.

'Sophia's' YouTube hero is Dan Pink delivering 'The Puzzle of Motivation' because of his ability to demonstrate humility through his intellect. She told me this was a rare ability, because it's so easy for people to punish others for being less clever than them.

Although 'Sophia' had collected many more sound bites on her voice recorder, these two stood out for me. I noticed a clear pattern, which led me to ask an impertinent question.

'Do you think you're smarter than the people you work with?'

'Oh goodness, no!' came the swift reply.

'Is the issue you're struggling with that you need a more comfortable way of voicing your expert opinion?' I asked.

'Yes, that's it. I find myself closing down at the very moment I should be speaking up.'

Through the observation exercise, 'Sophia' had self-discovered the most important combination for unlocking her business voice: how to come across as the expert in the room without sounding arrogant or, in her words, 'like a smarty pants'. She had seen others achieving this in a way she admired and wanted to emulate.

You might discover a completely different combination to 'Sophia'. That's the whole point of this case study; it shows the power of using your observations of what you admire in others to get to the truth of what you really need to develop.

Hint – you're not observing with the answer already in mind. I would urge you to be open-minded and follow your instincts and, dare I say, have some fun and enjoy it. At the end of the designated period, look for the most prominent trends in the people you've admired, specifically in the outcomes they've achieved rather than the techniques they've employed.

Now build on the exercise from Chapter 3 when I asked you to list your favourite speakers and isolate the outcome you most want to achieve from unlocking your business voice. You'll know you've nailed this section of the My Business Voice Methodology® when you can articulate this aim in a single sentence that can be understood by a friend in a social conversation. This clarity is vital to the rest of the work, so please don't go on until you've convinced yourself, otherwise the magic won't work.

One more thing – did you notice the vocal warm up at the beginning of the chapter?

'Beware Bandura's Bobo; beware Bandura's Bobo; beware Bandura's Bobo.'

Saying it three times quickly out loud is very good for getting those lips moving. When so much of the working day is governed by technology that sparks into life at the press of a few buttons, it's easy to forget that our own business machine needs a little more work to 'boot up'. That work is well worth it, though.

You are truly a multi-media wonder, and technology still has some way to go to catch up with you.

CHAPTER 7

Step 3: Intention

Are you chicken and rice or sugar and spice?

Have you ever prepared a presentation or speech and marvelled at your profundity and insight, only to find when you return to your work a short time before delivering it, the same content now sounds flat? My clients often tell me this can even happen during the presentation itself, setting their inner monologue into overdrive and resulting in the 'imposter' syndrome where they begin to doubt their credibility.

Even if you haven't experienced this phenomenon directly, the explanation of why it happens still holds the key to unlocking your business voice.

During real time communication, our brain automatically assigns intentions to our content. Intentions drive our message, giving it the light and shade that make it interesting to others and affecting our audience before the facts are scrutinised by them. That is not to say that decisions in business are made solely on the basis of feelings, but what is clear from nearly sixty years of research is that humans cannot switch off their emotions.

You may have been frustrated when you have attempted to replicate your own or somebody else's content without the original intentions. That's the moment you feel that something is missing; that the content seems less impactful than it did when you heard someone else delivering it. That's because there *is* something missing: your Recipe of Intention™.

For the purpose of creating your personalised recipe, your *Intention* is an actionable verb that will solicit a response from your audience. Specifically, intentions should be single words that can be prefixed by 'to'. Here are some examples:

- 💬 To reassure
- 💬 To update
- 💬 To thank

Here I will explain the concept of the Recipe of Intention and what I mean by the question 'Are you chicken and rice or sugar and spice?'

Imagine that your next evening meal will be plain chicken and rice (or, if you prefer, vegetables and rice). Will this meal keep you going? Of course it will. Now imagine that will be your evening meal for the next month. Will you still be alive at the end of the month? Yes, providing all the other necessities of life are in place.

My follow-up question is, 'How would you feel if I told you that you needed to follow the same diet for the next three months?' You wouldn't necessarily fear for your life; you'd have other meals to make up for lost nutrients or vitamins, but would you not feel pretty fed up with the predictability and blandness of what you were eating every evening?

Sometimes, inadvertently, this is how we make other people feel about our communication. Although our message contains the basic ingredients, it may be lacking the sugar and spice that will make us less predictable and more engaging.

During my time in the corporate world, I have attended many meetings that could have been headlined as 'chicken and rice' because they were heavy on the ingredients that seem to be the staple diet of intentions offered in meeting rooms around the world: to review. To update. To educate.

Permit me to follow the cooking metaphor one stage further. While every great sauce may start as a roux, it then needs an extra something to tickle the taste buds. The same is true with any piece of communication. We absolutely need to include the basic intentions, but have the courage to add some spice.

Here are some suggestions:

- 💬 To provoke
- 💬 To challenge
- 💬 To dazzle

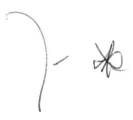

Can you spot the potential problem with having too many spicy intentions in your communication? The audience can quickly get overpowered by them and the content may lose its meaning. Likewise, if you've ever had to endure longer than a few minutes of being 'provoked, challenged and dazzled', you'll know that eventually the effect is dulled. So include some spicy intentions in your recipe, but use them sparingly.

Now complete your recipe by including some sugars – the intentions that literally sweeten the deal in any piece of communication, such as:

- 💬 To entertain
- 💬 To praise
- 💬 To flatter

Using sugars is not without risks. I've certainly listened to speakers who were all too keen on entertaining their audience, and then unfairly criticised for being more sizzle than substance. As with spices, a few 'sweeter' intentions go a long way.

The idea of adding intention to my content was the biggest learning point I took from drama school. Actors have to do this in order to create the original thoughts of the characters they play. Although unlocking your business voice has little to do with acting, this is one lesson I urge you to follow.

I understand that investing time in creating your own Recipe of Intention may seem obscure right now, but I urge you to try it. Strong intentions give power to the most mundane facts and figures. To help you, I've tabled some 'business voice' ingredient options to start things off.

MAIN INGREDIENTS	SPICES	SUGARS
Prepare	Excite	Amuse
Recommend	Shock	Inspire
Instigate	Warn	Welcome
Delegate	Accelerate	Reassure
Enlighten	Expose	Sparkle

I sneaked the not-so-corporate idea of sparkling in front of your audience at the end of my list, and I must credit my dear friend, mentor and partner in crime, Jonny, with opening my mind to non-corporate intentions. When he first suggested 'to sparkle' as a legitimate intention in business, I was cynical and thought it far too 'actory' for our mainly corporate clientele. But Jonny wasn't so easily put off and asked me if I'd ever presented an update about a project to share best practice with colleagues that had gone well. Now he was speaking my corporate language, and the answer was yes.

Then came his killer point: 'Did you take the opportunity to sparkle or did you just deliver the main ingredients?'

I had to think about it for a while, but came to the conclusion that he was right. On many such occasions, I hadn't seized the opportunity of adding a little sparkle to my delivery, and this had probably underplayed the achievement of the work I had done.

There's no guarantee, despite your best intentions, that the recipient of your presentation will be affected in the way you want them to be. There may be external factors that you can't control or perhaps aren't even aware of. However, remember that true confidence is generated by controlling what you can. Choosing your intention and committing to it absolutely falls into that category.

When you are clear about your intention, your content becomes much more potent and you can exert more influence by saying less, which will save you time and effort. The reverse is also true – if you're not sure about how you want others to feel and think, they'll fill in the blanks for you and create their own recipe. Often in the absence of clarity from the originator of the message, the recipient will assign less than favourable intentions and the outcome will be unsatisfactory for both sides.

I've seen this many times in practice. An example that stands out is when I worked with a newly appointed CEO who needed to address both the financial markets and the company's investors shortly after taking over the role. The mid-year position wasn't all that rosy, and the CEO was keen to manage the markets' expectations.

In the CEO's mind, this was a viable intention for their presentation. The problem I highlighted was that it was rather passive and therefore less likely to be received positively by the audience. In reality, any audience will feel it's *their* job to manage their expectations; they need something more front foot and active from the speaker to help them to reach a conclusion.

The CEO agreed to formulate a more active Recipe of Intention™ for their address to the markets and pulled it off by courageously calling the financial position early, then clarifying the story behind the numbers. They followed this with a confident challenge of traditional thinking in a rapidly changing economic climate, and ended with a reassurance that investing now would safeguard future performance.

The phrases that appeared most on the feedback collected after the speech were:

- Integrity, relating to the admission and calling it like it is
- Clarity, cutting through the detail to what was really going on
- Thought provoking, challenging and insightful
- A safe pair of hands to move the company forward

The audience commented most about how the new CEO's speech left them feeling. Of course, the content needed to pass heavy scrutiny, but the momentum of the speech was carried on the intentions – both the ingredients in the Recipe of Intention™ and the order in which they were added.

Exercise. Think about your next speech or presentation. What would your Recipe of Intention™ be? Imagine you've been limited to only five slides of content and that you need to assign a clear intention for each one. What journey will you take your audience on? What do you want them to be left feeling after they've forgotten what was actually written on your slides?

- Start with the main ingredients – what will be your intentions driving the facts?
- When and how will it be appropriate to spice things up a bit?
- What taste do you want to leave the audience with after your speech?

Take control of intentions when you communicate, particularly during conversations, presentations and speeches that matter. Start by thinking about your Recipe of Intention, balancing the main ingredients with sugar and spices.

It's all too easy for audiences to zone out from presentations that are 'stodgy' with updates and information. Really think about how you want to affect your audience and build your content around that. Don't fall into the trap of recycling content or a previous slide deck that more or less fits the brief; that will only lead to the content not working as well as you'd hoped.

To unlock your business voice, unlock the power of intention and build your content to match your recipe.

CHAPTER 8

Step 4: Casting

Who you need to be

By the time I had graduated from drama school and been taken on by my first agent, the die had already been cast (a long time ago, as it happens). In my head, I would have been an awesome James Bond and given Sean Connery (and everyone who followed) a run for their money, but in reality that didn't count. It was how the world saw me that truly mattered, and that turned out to be good news. In my late thirties, I had to come to terms with the fact that I would never play James Bond or be the romantic lead. I just wasn't in that casting mould.

In the acting profession, you quickly become aware of how the world sees you because that is the work you get offered. I was fortunate to have a fantastic agent who knew exactly which roles to put me forward for. In my case, what I have for free (courtesy of genetics) is a deep and resonant voice that belies my short stature and has landed me a variety of roles, from a medieval priest to a barrister, to a slightly psychopathic CEO.

My agent was helpful in making me focus on what I could use, rather than chasing what I'd never be. This is a great lesson in business. The likelihood is you have assigned 'castings' to your colleagues, albeit subconsciously, and they have done the same to you. These castings are not fixed; they change with time and depending on your role. However, there will be natural limits to how far you can stretch your natural casting. You can't break the mould you were made with, so be aware of those limits, work within them, and it will be very good news for you, too.

There is a good chance that, like mine was, your initial perception of how you come across to others will be biased by your internal filters. The reticular activating system (RAS) is located at the base of our brains, and amongst other functions, it is responsible for filtering the overwhelming amount of information that bombards us every waking hour. The RAS is in fact our own personal search engine and has a tendency to delete, distort and generalise the information at our disposal.

With this in mind (literally), I strongly recommend that you focus on the external evidence rather than your own perceptions. This evidence is how other people who know you would describe you. However, you need to be wary of the Observer Effect, which suggests that our behaviours change as a result of being observed. This means that when you ask someone to observe you and then comment on what they see, two people's behaviours are likely to be affected: yours and theirs.

To neutralise this effect and give structure to how others provide useful insights from what they observe, I've come up with four questions you can ask colleagues to monitor:

- Are people clear about my views and opinions?
- What's the trust level in my impartiality?
- Do I come across as a good listener?
- Can I excite people with my ideas?

Ask people to rank your performance against each question. An arbitrary scale of 1–10 will help you to work out the natural preferences in your communication style and areas you can work on in the final section of the My Business Voice Methodology®: *Experiment*. Specifically, these questions will uncover where your dials are currently set for the fundamental components of your communication, namely:

- Your level of assertiveness
- Whether you speak more in facts or feelings
- How well you tune in to others

These observations (or 'data points' in business speak) minimise the Observer Effect because you're asking people to comment on the effect of your communication rather than pick up on individual behavioural traits and habits. This is much more useful to you, as you won't unlock your business voice by temporarily working on the habits you've developed over the years. You will achieve your goals by aligning what you work on with the effect you need to have on others when you speak.

The theory behind this, and the idea that we all have preferences in terms of our communication style, has been with us a very long time indeed. As far back as 460–370 BC, Hippocrates incorporated the four humours of choleric, sanguine, phlegmatic and melancholic into his medical theories. Although modern medicine has long since dismissed the medical application of personality types, psychologists have taken up the mantle. During my research for this book, I lost count after discovering at least thirty different variations on this theme.

Two of my favourites will help add weight to the practical aspects and value of understanding natural *Casting*. The first is *People Styles At Work* written by Robert and Dorothy Bolton. I applaud their work because it focuses on how to flex your natural style to be more comfortable to people with other preferences. In the appendices, there is a section for each of the four styles they describe with great tips on how to adapt to the others. I particularly like their directive to choose a couple of things that come relatively easily to you rather than attempt a personality transplant to fit in with the crowd.

My second is *Who Moved My Cheese?* by Dr Spencer Johnson. The book is not long; Dr Johnson has also written children's books, so his message is easy to digest, but if you don't have time to read the book, please find ten minutes or so to watch one of the several YouTube videos of the same title.

Strictly speaking, the core message of the book is how to deal with change rather than understanding your natural casting in terms of communication style. However, the next and final part of the model, *Experiment*, is about overcoming the fear of trying different ways to get your message across, and that is why the fable of the four characters' quest for the cheese is so inspirational.

Most importantly of all, rejoice in what you get for free, especially in terms of your natural communication style. It's exactly why people like interacting with you. Having a clear appreciation of what others value in how you come across to them is vital to unlocking your business voice because it will feed your confidence in difficult situations. I know from working with hundreds of clients over the years that the most common reason for them getting tongue tied, and therefore 'locked and blocked' at work, is underestimating what they already have at their disposal. If you're not sure, use the four questions to find out before you look to do anything else.

I'm going to end this chapter where I started, with what I learnt from my first agent and my early attempts to eke out a career in show business. Far from limiting your opportunities, knowing and appreciating the limits of your natural casting (how others see you) will give you the security and freedom to push the boundaries and make more of an impact. It worked for me.

CHAPTER 9

Step 5: Experiment

Be safe, not sorry

You've probably heard the maxim about regretting what we don't try rather than what we do. I subscribe to this belief, and would add that we are much more likely to push our boundaries if we've invested some time on self-research and rehearsal in a safe environment.

Don't underestimate the power of labelling the things that hold you back. Calling out your concerns gives you back control, and your fears will not seem so paralysing when you put some boundaries around them. After you've done this, it's less about 'reframing', which implies rework or moving backwards, and more about letting go and moving on.

In this final stage of the My Business Voice Methodology®, I'll ask you to pull together your discoveries from the work you've done so far and formulate your experimental method. That way, you'll make the most of whatever resources you can spare.

During my days as a chemistry student, my favourite teacher was very hot on having a clear plan before throwing anything into a test tube. I'd like to share with you his (good-humoured) warning: 'Don't be a bucket chemist.' In other words, don't chuck a few things in and hope you'll get the reaction you want.

The 'Parallel Universe' is a wonderful place. Providing you stick to its statute regarding morality, legality and ethics, you can say whatever you like, however you like. There are no permanent consequences to what you say or how you say it in the Parallel Universe.

Although you won't find it on any celestial map, the Parallel Universe is a place that you can easily create with your imagination. Consequently, it is the perfect place to experiment and try things out without fear of failure. You'll only truly know where to set your internal dials in any given situation if you practise in the Parallel Universe and discover the too highs and the too lows.

117

The metaphor of the internal dial is to make it clear that this part of the methodology is all about fine-tuning what you've got rather than attempting to flick a switch and stick on techniques that aren't right for you. I've seen people attempt to make the latter work, and usually they end up in a worse place than where they started. In the next chapter, I'll take you through the implementation of the My Business Voice Methodology®, but for now, I want to give you a blueprint for how to rehearse and try things out. It's not as straightforward as you may think.

Time is the most precious resource at our disposal. Ultimately, none of us truly know how much of it we have got, and not everyone gets the same amount. That's why everyone on the planet agonises over how to spend it.

Experimenting with how you communicate is time well spent, because it will enable you to grow professionally and in confidence throughout the rest of your career. Through my work, I've been privileged to see how the careers of my clients have progressed over the years that I've worked with them. What I commonly observe is the transition from technical and knowledge expert to influencer and implementer. This is all about leadership. However, that's almost too simplistic, because my clients tell me it's much more about discovering a new anchor for their competence and confidence.

In other words, career progression is less about relying on knowing more than your peers and more about developing executive gravitas through your vocal presence on the business stage. However, let me 'bust the Bard' (William Shakespeare) just a bit by clarifying that not all the world (of business) is in fact a stage. Otherwise, we would be rehearsing every meeting, every call and every email, and we certainly don't have time for that. What will work much better is to make a choice about the next meeting, call or presentation that is important enough to spend our time rehearsing.

A great coach gets out of the way of their client. I truly believe that my chief responsibility as a coach is to be there to facilitate good rehearsal and encourage experimentation. My aim in writing this book is to act as your catalyst and motivator to start this work.

I also know that self-help books have their limitations, one of which is that they can never talk back. Finding a like-minded buddy to work with you on unlocking your business voice will greatly increase both the speed and the consistency of your progress. This isn't a new insight, but experience tells me that very few of my clients have made use of their peer group buddy network because they don't know where to start. It can feel a bit weird if you've never tried it before, but take some risks, invest the time to find a buddy and then choose the right time and environment to experiment.

As obvious as it may sound, you need an agenda for a rehearsal session, the same way you would create one for any other important meeting. That's why I've included an example at the end of the chapter of what you might work on. Whether you hire a coach or continue this work with a buddy, make sure you're clear on what you want to work on and don't bite off too much at once.

Why did such obvious considerations make it into this book? It's because they are the simple things that people often don't pay attention to, and then they wonder why they can't unlock the business voice they need and want. I'm not too proud to admit that in my early days as a coach, I was less particular about the right agenda, time and place for my client sessions. When I look back now, by making it too easy for my clients, I was devaluing their work.

I can remember turning up to coaching appointments when my client's head was full of what was coming their way later that day, or being crammed into a tiny meeting room with glass walls and the rest of the office looking in. All that really happened during these appointments was a bit of theory and some chit-chat. Not surprisingly, now I insist on having a clear agenda, a time slot when heads can be relatively clear, and an appropriate space. The results are so much better and less frustrating for all concerned.

If you can't commit to that at the very least, then you'll be wasting your time and energy – and those of your coach or buddy.

The final part of the My Business Voice Methodology® combines the preceding components to give you the aim, variables and process to conduct your business voice experiments. You'll need to look back over the previous exercises to create your plan and discover the formula to unlock your business voice.

- Choose a realistic outcome for your communication

- What do you admire in others that you can make your own?

- How will you mix your Recipe of Intention™ to drive your content?

- Where can you exploit and stretch your natural casting?

- Who can you ask to be your rehearsal buddy?

Use this template as an example.

VOCATION – my new role requires me to contribute to strategic and therefore potentially ambiguous conversations, as well as share my expertise and knowledge.

OBSERVATION – I need to be better at grabbing impromptu moments to go off-piste when I present at leadership meetings and be more comfortable sharing my opinions.

INTENTION – I want to spice up my Recipe of Intention™ with a bit more challenging and provoking and counter this with some reassuring and inspiring, leaving out any trace of apologising.

CASTING – to the outside world, I may come across as empathetic, considered and a safe pair of hands. It would be even better if people saw me as an assertive thought leader.

EXPERIMENT – my target is the next monthly Senior Leadership Team meeting, and I'm going to ask 'Sam' to practise with me and challenge my views on the new procurement process.

You'll know you've worked the methodology correctly if you can distil your plan to this degree of clarity. That's not to say that you can shortcut the process, so if you get to this stage but you're still unclear, go back and work through it again.

You will get results if you have a clear VOICE in your head and in writing before you start. In Part 3, I'll help you to take your voice out of the lab and into the field.

It's time to swap the lab coat for the power suit.

PART 3

Translating Theory Into Practice And Performance

CHAPTER 10

First Aid For Common Communication Ailments

There's something intensely irritating about a well-crafted model that easily lifts off the page when you read it, but doesn't offer any suggestions of how to translate the plausible theory into results in the real world. I'm not going to leave you in that predicament.

In this section, you'll have the opportunity to link the My Business Voice Methodology® to the situations that are relevant to your world of work. However, since there are common communication ailments in all businesses, it's worth your while exploring all the variants that I'll show you.

I'm always delighted when my clients want to stay and chat at the end of a workshop, and often I'm asked to comment on a specific issue they're experiencing back at their office. These conversations frequently start something like this: 'The situation is rather complicated, so please bear with me while I take you through the background.'

My primary job at this point is to listen; there's enough good therapy in that alone. However, the situation is hardly ever just down to the 'background', otherwise the same strategy wouldn't work in so many different cases. It's usually much more to do with the quality and clarity of the communication the client has with their colleagues, particularly in meetings, presentations and during conference calls.

In 2013, the Katzenbach Center at Strategy& surveyed senior global executives and revealed that only 54% of major change initiatives in business were successful. That's shockingly low, given the frequency of change nowadays and the time and money companies invest to get change embedded. One of the major contributors to failure that the survey identified was a lack of engagement caused by poor communication. There is plenty to suggest that locked voices have a real and measurable cost in business.

Here is a link to the survey: www.strategyand.pwc.com/reports/cultures-role-organizational-change

This is a pertinent moment to remind you that the messages you form in your mind are made visual to others through your body and given meaning by the instrument that is your voice. Whenever you communicate at work, it happens through an integrated system combining your *mind*, *body* and *voice*.

From now on, think of all three as part of your business hardware. Therefore, they are in need of maintenance and updating in the same way as all the other business machines you depend on to do your job effectively. With that in mind (and, of course, body and voice), I have included some drills and routines to help you warm up your business machine and keep it in tip-top working order.

I know only too well from my own experience, and from working with my clients, that if you don't achieve some early quick wins, it's very hard to persevere with a long range plan. Unlocking your business voice is no different, and that is why I'm going to offer you some tactical tools and help you to solve the niggling communication ailments you may already be experiencing at work.

Playing the status game

You may have noticed how reason and logic seem to lose their potency when faced with the abrupt misuse of power and authority by others. I've seen my clients struggle with this time and time again. Their resolve crumbles in front of others they perceive as having a higher status than them. At this point, all the preparation and rehearsal they've done feels like it counts for nothing and their inner monologue is yelling at them to retreat, accept the inevitable and live another day.

On other occasions, they may go to the opposite extreme and over-inflate their own status in an attempt to match the other person's, only to come across as a petulant and rebellious child. Either way, they become easy to dismiss and their message doesn't get heard.

This sense of 'status mismatch' is one of the primary communication ailments found in every type of business. It's also one of the main reasons people lose faith in their work without managing to unlock their business voice.

The problem lies with how others use (or abuse) their status, and this seems to be out of our control. After all, we're not them, so how can we influence them to 'play nicely'? What's actually happening is that the other person (or people) has influenced *us* and made us turn our status dial down or up. That's one thing we can do something about.

The dictionary definition of 'status' is pretty clear:

1.   A social or professional position, condition or standing

2.   The relative position or standing of a person; stature of a champion

COLLINS DICTIONARY AND THESAURUS, PUB. 2000

My contention is that this definition is not as simple as it seems, and here's why. During my workshops, I'll ask the group what status at work means to them and collect their thoughts on a flipchart.

Here's a typical outcome:

- Job title/rank/grade
- Hierarchy
- Power/influence

At first glance, there doesn't appear to be anything noteworthy from what's on the flipchart. It's a fairly predictable line up, much like the dictionary definition. However, if you combine the two, the result is a list of things out of your control – position, standing, job title, rank, grade and hierarchy. Of course, they do move with time, but in the immediate situation you're in, they are pretty much fixed.

Or are they? Look again at the two definitions – what's critically missing? Stature of a champion, power/influence and inner and outer. I get excited when I read 'stature of a champion' tagged on to the second dictionary definition; it's easily missed, because it sounds like something you *can* control. This is where you regain control and manage your status, rather than being defeated by other people.

I'm always delighted when the group makes the distinction between the power/influence they have in the moment and their standing in the company hierarchy. When I drop a few hints, most groups will volunteer the idea that they can feel low status on the inside and still project a relatively high status on the outside.

Projecting the right status for you, given the specific situation and the other people involved, is exactly the right place to start. When others of a higher status in the company hierarchy aren't playing nicely, you need to work from the outside (your body and voice) to get the inside (your mindset) to join up.

To demonstrate this in my workshops, I perform an exercise that seems a bit odd when I first describe it. I ask the group to sit in a horseshoe facing the door of the training room. Next, I'll explain that I'm going to come into the room ten times, and on each occasion the content of what I say will be exactly the same: 'Hello, my name is Simon.'

I ask a colleague or a participant with a loud voice to count me in, one to ten. The ten occasions run quickly, one after another, so that there's only a heartbeat between me leaving the room as #1 (having delivered my content) and then re-entering the room as #2, and so on until I get to #10. The group is tasked with writing down a single word for each occasion (#1–10) that best describes the impression each 'Simon' made on them.

The results are always consistent. This list, shared by a recent participant, is representative of what I get.

1. Weird
2. Embarrassed
3. Worried
4. Unsure
5. Tentative
6. Open-minded
7. Confident
8. Welcoming
9. Cocky
10. Arrogant

From this list of words, what's happening to my status on the ten occasions I enter the room? It goes from too low, heads towards about right, and then accelerates over the top and arrives at too much.

I then ask the group a deliberately subjective question: 'Which one of the ten versions would you most like to say hello to?' Out of the hundreds of times I've run this exercise in a workshop, I can only remember a few #9s and the odd #5. Almost without exception, the answers are #6, #7, or most frequently #8. Note, it's not my content that's altering my status, since it's restricted and is the same for each of the ten versions. What I am changing is my use of the space, as well as the volume, pitch and pace of my voice and my body shape, to make the transition from low to high status.

When I carried out this exercise with a group of IT business partners in Germany and had just made the distinction between what you can change that will affect your status versus what you can't, one of the participants offered some rather personal advice.

'Well, you could go to the gym and get more exercise.'

This line cut deeply because it was delivered without any venomous intent. It was more like a statement of absolute fact. My only response was that it wouldn't have much effect in the time between each of the ten versions of me coming into the room, but I'd bear it in mind for the future.

There is a video of this exercise on my YouTube Channel under the 'Moments of Truth' playlist, which you can access via www.myfirsttrainers.com.

To make this helpful to you right now, here is a summary of the behaviours demonstrated during the exercise, split by the high or low status response you will get from your audience.

Self-sabotaging low status behaviours:

WHAT IT LOOKS LIKE	WHAT IT DOES
Hardly entering the room before speaking	Allows the space to own you
Using the door or furniture as a crutch	Increases the tension in your body
Making your frame appear smaller	Closes down your body, then your mind
Lack of connecting eye contact	Limits the connection with your audience
Upward inflection at the end of sentences	Turns your statements into questions
Speaking too fast and not leaving pauses	Lowers the importance of your content

Self-supporting high status behaviours:

WHAT TO DO	WHAT THE EFFECT IS
Enter the room on an in-breath	Lungs full of air will make you float
Plant both feet before you speak	Brings the picture of you into focus
Risk a smile and make an early connection	Invites your audience into your message
Check in with your eyes	No need to stare, but let them see you care
Start with short sentences	Helps maintain the power of your voice
Leave appropriate pauses	The audience keeps up with your thinking

The feeling of being slightly undermined and not able to get your message across is debilitating. Take confidence and reassurance that your status is in your own hands and you can do something to limit the effect of that feeling.

Next time it happens, here's what to do:

Label your unhelpful belief. Be specific about the situation and people – for example, 'Speaking at the ExCo worries me because I could look stupid'.

Replace that belief with something else that you know is true. For example, 'I will know about the project and that's what the audience will be interested in'.

Qualify the status of the other people in the meeting #1–10. Take a reflective rather than an emotional view to get to the reality of the situation.

Establish the scale of your own status. For example, 'The lowest I've dropped before would be #4, and the highest I'm realistically capable of carrying off is #8'.

Make a choice about the specific # you'll be in the meeting. There's no right or wrong answer. You're already more in control by choosing what will serve you best.

Finally, practise using the high status (and self-supporting) behaviours when you rehearse your presentation, speech, or even just your opening comments. It's crucial that you make a definite choice that you're at peace with beforehand, so that you can anchor the right behaviours and thereby set your business machine – mind, body and voice – to be ready to deliver.

How to avoid networking nightmares

What do you say to people you don't know? Most of us worry about waffling in front of relative strangers, even in friendly surroundings like at internal company away days. From your side, what if you get stuck talking to the same people and miss out on making a connection that would really make a difference?

I was inspired by what happened to my closest friend from school. Simon (having the same name as me isn't my prerequisite for selecting friends) recently moved firms within the same industry, and in fact the same niche area. In Property, there's still very much a tradition of whom you know as well as what you know. Simon had always been aware of that during his fifteen-year tenure with his previous employer.

His move to a much bigger and, in his own words, 'more corporate' player meant that he needed to establish himself and raise his profile quickly in order to benefit from the firm's large internal referral network. The problem was that Simon absolutely hated networking. From our many previous conversations, I'd gathered that he'd attended numerous external events, and although he'd survived, he'd come away with an abject fear of small talk – or rather, of running out of it. In Simon's mind, networking with others from within his own company would be even worse, because 'that's what people do at company away days'.

What I really admired about him was that he knew he needed to do it, and that creating a process he felt comfortable with would help. After all, that would be his approach to handling a rating on a new site.

Simon and I worked together, and what we came up with worked so well, he even shared it with his wife. Now you too can use the 'SAS' (Simon and Simon) approach to avoiding networking nightmares.

Get your name right! It's amazing how easy it is to get your name stuck in your throat when you're nervous. The truth is that you don't say it out loud as often as you may think. Other people do it when they introduce you and probably give it more care than you do.

Facts, not fluff. Make the first thing you tell others easy to digest, because at this point people aren't interested in a clever spin on how you earn a living. In my case, telling people that I'm a Voice Unlocker is ambiguous and just wastes time. I'm a Presentation and Public Speaking Coach. That way they know where I fit, which is how our brains like to work.

This is my niche. Tell people what you specialise in. For example, 'I specialise in working with technical experts who often regard themselves as reflective and introverted.' Your niche can be a group of people, a location or a specific area of work.

Limiting the scope of the conversation is a good thing, because it reassures your audience that they won't need to spend a lot of their time working out if you're useful to them.

'I truly believe that...' Finish off with a personal decision you've made about what you do. In my case, it would be, 'Everyone's best version of themselves is always good enough'. It doesn't need to be earth-shatteringly insightful or delivered with the belief and passion of a prophet; that's not the point. The real power lies in the notion that decision makers prefer making decisions with other decision makers. Finishing with a personal statement will prove your proficiency in this respect.

The content you attach to this framework should be delivered in no more than a handful of sentences, which should be possible to recite on one really good belly breath. Also, like any good brochure or piece of marketing, it should encourage more questions.

Here are my top tips for using your social pitch out in the field.

Practise saying your name. Say it three times as fast as you can, immediately followed by three times at half the pace of normal speech. Without thinking about it, then say your name normally. For some reason, this exercise resets everything so that you say your name at the correct pace and intensity for people you haven't met before. Obviously, don't do this in front of someone; that really would be weird. However, it is a great warm-up exercise for somewhere private before you enter the arena.

Approach groups of people you want to join with physical energy. There's no need to bound and leap over; instead, aim for the urgency you'd naturally have when walking to meet a friend you hadn't seen for a while. Focus on the person in the group who is speaking as you approach. Smile, but do not attempt to interrupt them. It's likely they will at least return the smile or acknowledge you in some way.

Everyone else will see them doing this and will accept you into the group.

Leaving groups can be tricky too. There's no need for gimmicks like pretending you need the toilet or another drink. Everyone is there for the same reason, so when appropriate, thank the person or people for something specific. For example, 'I enjoyed hearing about the applications of virtual reality in biotech', not something facile like, 'Thanks for your time, great to meet you'. This proves you've actually been listening and gives you a licence to leave the group without apologising.

At his first company offsite meeting, my friend Simon made an important contract with himself. Before setting off, he promised that he would talk to everybody he didn't know at some point during the day. Don't forget, Simon hates networking, but now he had a plan that he'd practised and knew was fit for purpose.

That weekend we met for a catch up and I immediately noticed how good Simon felt about how the event had gone. It was obvious that giving it a go had boosted his confidence even before we'd talked about how it went. In typical Simon style, his account was factual, pragmatic and low on hype; he'd become more fluent as the day had progressed, and there were some people that he'd connected with more than others, but his big win was finally realising that setting realistic expectations and practising being his best self were the ways to avoid networking nightmares. It was a classic win-win as Simon paid for our curry that evening as a thank you for my help.

141

You can use this framework to create your own social pitch. Try it and refine it at every opportunity you have.

Coping with conflict

Have you noticed contrasting attitudes towards conflict amongst your colleagues, friends and family, and how different people deal with it? Some people will equate conflict with stress; others with excitement and the potential for progress. This is hardly surprising, as the physical manifestations of stress and excitement are more or less the same. Our heart rate increases, as does our breathing, and our major (movement) muscles get an energy turbo-charge in readiness for whatever challenge is ahead.

What everybody tends to agree on, irrespective of their view of conflict, is that it can be hard to give a good account of themselves and get across what they actually mean. From many years of coaching my clients for these challenging encounters, I've found the potential for misunderstanding during conflict is significant. At best this can waste time and unnecessarily prolong decision making; at worst, people may say something that they later regret.

These are not the only immediate physical complications to deal with. The other party's communication is also likely to be 'overly spicy' in the context of their Recipe of Intention™. In other words, no matter how many deep breaths you take to remain calm, you still need to address the intensity of the communication coming from them, which may be heavily laced with emotion.

When you encounter conflict, it can often feel like you and the other party are talking different languages. Even if tempers remain intact, the speed and intensity of the communication increases, and if you're not prepared for it, mistakes and miscommunication are the likely outcome. Sadly, I've lost count of the times clients have told me, 'If only I'd said...' or 'Why didn't I think of that at the time, instead of five steps along the corridor?' Taking a deep breath to compose yourself is a really good start, but that will only get you so far.

Here's what to do when your conflict receptors are triggered:

Use colleagues' own words (UCOW). This is frequently noted on my workshop feedback sheet to key my memory. It simply means prove you've listened by repeating back what you've just heard.

Examples I've heard from my clients include:

- You don't have the knowledge or experience to spot the pitfalls in this
- Everything your department touches goes wrong
- It's not as simple as you're claiming, there's much more going on

Obviously, you need to precede the repeat back with something like, 'What you're saying is...' Be careful to deliver this without venom or emotion, which I appreciate can be difficult if what the other party has said started with one of the classics like 'With all due respect', which actually means no respect at all. Instead, speak as if you're repeating directions you've just received from a stranger.

143

There is a little gift embedded in this first piece of advice. Watch what happens when you do this. The other person is very likely to nod in agreement as you repeat back what they've just said.

Be curious and use your TED. Once both sides have established what the headline issue is, it's then much safer and far less predictable to be curious rather than conflicting. Avoid the overworked business cliché 'that's interesting' if that's not what you think. Your insincerity will be spotted straight away. Instead, use your TED: tell, explain or describe.

- 'Tell me a bit more about (that)' works well with direct people, who will tell it as it is

- 'Explain exactly when/what/how...' is better for more analytical and detailed types

- 'Describe what that feels like' releases the emotions that have got bottled up

This uncomplicated invitation helps both sides of any conflict. The other party will mark your courage in exploring the issue further and is more likely to acknowledge whatever solution you offer later on in the debate. You will know more about what's really at stake and therefore avoid making assumptions. Stay curious and don't make any judgments yet.

Mind the gap. I've covered how people like to play the status game at work by raising theirs and attempting to lower yours (and what to do about it) earlier in this chapter. Conflict is a great platform for those who enjoy this sport and exaggerate the gap between their status and yours to gain the advantage. Don't be distracted by others who use their business machine – mind, body and voice – to undermine your status. Instead, match and mirror what they're doing rather than competing in trying to dominate and win.

There are some tricks for doing this:

- Remain upright and open, without puffing out your chest like a bodybuilder
- Position yourself on a slight angle rather than directly opposite the other party
- Mirror the length of their sentences, particularly in the early exchanges
- Match their vocal intensity, not their volume, and speak one beat slower than them

When you mind the gap, and remain within range of the other party, no matter how senior they are, any discussion is likely to be in the adult to adult category. Adults have differences of opinion and are prepared to debate the outcome and move on without scoring points. Eliminating conflict would be detrimental to business because it would hamper progress; we all just need to be grown-up about it.

In this chapter, I've offered you practical advice on the three most common scenarios that get talked about in my coaching sessions and workshops:

- Managing status, yours and other people's
- Introducing yourself at networking events
- Coping with conflict

I'm sure you don't need any help noticing when situations could have gone better. The evidence is always there: progress is slow and relationships suffer. What is harder and takes more courage is changing something in the moment and trusting that the outcome will be different, at the very least. When you do this, you'll always learn something.

The way to unlock your business voice is by small trials, including the occasional error. To cement this idea, I want to take you back to my days in the Territorial Army, roaming the Brecon Beacons with a map and compass. Before letting me loose on the hills, the Regiment I was training with taught me the theory of map reading in the comfort of the barracks. However, the most important instruction I received in that warm and dry classroom was actually about getting lost.

Any quest in life is not about avoiding getting lost; it's much more about noticing when you do get lost and making small corrections to steer yourself back on course. Even retracing your steps and starting from a secure point is better than carrying on regardless.

In short, you don't need to make radical changes to unlock your business voice, but you do need to believe that practice and persevering with real situations will get you there eventually.

CHAPTER 11

Low Drama No Excuse Warm-up

To help you unlock your business voice so it's ready to use before you start, I am going to offer you some quick and easy ways to get yourself in the zone for moment-of-truth meetings and presentations.

I regard myself as a hybrid of the science and art communities, which has, on occasions, made life a bit more stressful than it needs to be for me. My time at drama school is a good example of this – the hours I spent lying on the floor in a draughty rehearsal room, desperately trying to connect to my centre, while imagining breathing through my knees. Rather frustratingly, the left side of my brain, which prefers logic to Rock 'n' Roll, wouldn't quite allow my imagination to set me free. I did, however, respect my Russian movement teacher and understand the need to prepare for the heightened state required to make an impact on stage as an actor. This led me to develop a warm-up routine that incorporated her wisdom while remaining outside the boundaries of what I consider a bit 'actor wanky'. That way there was a good chance that I would actually do it and reap the benefits without getting bogged down in the drama.

I'll share with you the mechanics of what I do, and I have also created a video, 'Low Drama No Excuse Warm-up', on my YouTube channel, which you can access via www.myfirsttrainers.com. As well as the physiological benefits of doing a personal warm-up, the psychological effect is equally important.

The psychological benefit of a self-care routine was evident during my time as a soldier. I noticed that more experienced 'squaddies' would often brush their teeth on exercise, i.e. out in the field, whenever there was a break, irrespective of the time of day. I was curious, so asked why they did this. One of my NCOs told me that it gave them a lift when they were feeling like they'd had enough – 'on your chinstraps' was the phrase in vogue at the time. I tried it next time I was feeling like that, and there was something about the simplicity and privacy of the ritual that really worked.

I've convinced many sceptical clients to invest some of their time in warming up before important meetings and presentations by using a sporting analogy. For example, I doubt you'd limber up every morning in preparation for walking around the office; after all, it's routine and something you do every day. However, if you visit the gym, there's a fair chance you'll do a few stretches because your body will be put under more stress than normal.

Unlocking your business voice is no different to exercising, because being on your feet presenting puts additional stress on your body – not least your vocal cords, which are literally pressed into action, talking for extended periods, projecting and enunciating. I'm not expecting you to warm up and stretch before every conference call or update meeting, but there will be times when you know you're going to be under more stress than normal. In these situations, five minutes of warming up will be as important as the hours you've put into preparing your content.

So, here's my three-step Low Drama No Excuse Warm-up for getting 'on stage' ready:

- Tense and release
- Connect the breath
- Engage your resonators

Before you start, find somewhere out of the way and private. If your presentation or meeting is first thing in the morning, you can do this at home before you leave.

This is what to do.

Tense and release. The objective for the next couple of minutes is to unlock any tension that is trapped in your body. You may not be aware that you're holding tension; it happens subconsciously when your mind gets anxious and tells your body to prepare for flight or fight. By making your body smaller, for example by closing down the

151

space between your arms and legs, you appear less confident to your audience. Your brain reacts to this closed physical state by increasing the level of cortisol, which is associated with stress.

Take off your shoes, so that you can feel the floor, and remove any clothing that will restrict your movement, for example a jacket, tie or belt. Starting with your feet, gently but firmly tense and release them three times, one at a time. The easiest way to tense your feet is to curl your toes downwards without moving your ankle. After you've done this three times, allow your foot to go limp at the ankle and enjoy a bit of a shake and release from the knee downwards.

Repeat this tense and release trilogy for the rest of your body in this order:

- Ankles
- Calves
- Knees
- Buttocks
- Hips
- Hands
- Arms
- Shoulders
- Face

These warm-up exercises are influenced by the basics of Pilates and Yoga. The crucial purpose of this first stage of tense and relax is to release any locked stress hiding in your body. Give it a try, and afterwards check in with yourself and observe if you feel any different. I'm willing to bet you'll probably feel just a little bit brighter, and perhaps even a bit taller.

This routine is what works for me, and that is exactly the point. Here are a few tips for developing your own warm-up routine:

- Invest in each exercise and focus your attention on that part of your body
- Mix up your movements; round and round as well as up and down
- Maximise the space your body fills; expand your chest and stretch out your limbs
- Don't forget to shake out after each set of three
- Remember this is a warm-up, not an exercise class; be gentle with yourself

My absolute favourite part of this ritual is combining 'jazz hands' with 'jazz face' – that wide-eyed and cheesy grin look; for some reason I find it almost impossible to do one without the other. I guess my movement teacher had an effect after all!

Connect the breath. Another common reaction to stress and anxiety is shallow breathing. As the term suggests, this means that your breath is focused around your throat; you take in less air and so you need to breathe more often. This has the knock-on effect of making you sound like you're gabbling as your vocal cords tighten, and the pitch of your voice also heightens – i.e. you start to squeak your words. Talking too fast and at too high a pitch are both associated with nerves and lower status behaviour, and when your inner monologue notices you doing this, the nerves can really kick in. At this point, it's all too easy to get caught in a downward spiral and go into 'get it over with' survival mode.

The best fuel for unlocking your business voice comes from your diaphragm, and connecting your breath from there is a perfect place to start. Your diaphragm is a dome-shaped sheet of muscle and tendon that separates your chest from your abdomen.

Firstly, work out exactly where your diaphragm is. It's not as obvious as it may sound, because most of the time you don't pay much attention to it. Here's a quick way of finding your diaphragm.

Stand in front of a mirror and place your right hand on your stomach so that the tip of your thumb is resting just below the end of your sternum (breastbone). Now breathe in as deeply as you can, watching yourself in the mirror and trying to keep your shoulders as still as possible. As you inhale, you should feel your hand being pushed out as your lungs expand and fill with air. As you exhale, you'll notice your hand being sucked back into its original position.

Repeat this three times and challenge yourself to increase the movement of your hand each time, both the rise and the fall. Release your shoulders followed by a shake down; you've earnt it, and you'll be ready for part two.

For part two, you need to be alone in a space where you won't be overheard. Either that, or with people you don't mind looking a bit silly in front of, because I'm going to ask you to repeat the above exercise, only on the exhale impersonate a neighing horse.

To get the maximum benefit, you'll really need to go for it. Commit to neighing and it won't be as silly as it sounds. Again, keeping the shoulders still on the inhale, force the air back out and make your lips vibrate as fast and for as long as you can. The advanced version of this exercise (yes, there is one) involves moving up and down your natural scale, from the lowest bass note to the highest. Again, I demonstrate this exercise on the Low Drama No Excuse Warm-up video on my YouTube channel.

Once you get over the ridiculousness of doing this, you may find it becomes a bit addictive. I sometimes spoil myself at the end of the final neigh by breaking into a rather bad *Scooby-Doo* impression. However, much more important is what this exercise does. It connects your breath to your diaphragm and encourages you to fuel your voice properly; the better and longer the neigh, the more fuel you've taken on board.

In normal speech, this increases your control considerably and means you can vary the pitch, pace and volume of your voice more easily. The other benefit is that this exercise loosens your jaw and lips, which means that you're more likely to open your mouth properly when you speak. This is massively important, because the action and intent behind your content is delivered by the verbs, and verbs are full of vowels. Getting your point across will mean articulating between vowels, and your jaw and lips will need to be ready for that challenge.

While you're in front of the mirror, sound out the vowels A-E-I-O-U and you'll see what I mean. Notice the range of mouth movement needed to make them clear.

You're now ready to engage your voice and complete the warm up.

Engage your resonators. I'm often asked by my clients for advice on how to project their voice better so that it carries in larger spaces and to bigger audiences. The common misconception is that the only way to be heard is to raise the volume by pushing and straining. This is not true; your body is built for resonance, and if you allow your sound to build in your natural hollows, your voice will carry without stress or strain. Volume and vocal quality are not the same thing; volume can easily be increased with amplification, while the quality of your voice cannot.

Your final task, therefore, is to engage with your natural resonating chambers and pull your voice forward from the back of your throat, where it can get stuck, to the front of your face. Humming is your access code, and that's where it starts. Head back to the mirror, take a deep diaphragm breath and exhale on a steady hum. The aim is to make both lips vibrate vigorously so that you can only just prevent them from parting. You'll probably feel a bit of a tickling sensation.

Once you've mastered humming on the lips, open the hum out into a 'Mar'. As you do this, your jaw will open in the vertical plane. You'll know you're opening your mouth wide enough if you can stick your index and middle fingers between your lips as you do it. Repeat several times and explore your resonating chambers by gently tapping your palm around your upper chest. Then on another cycle, place both hands on the top of your head.

You'll hear and feel the effect of tapping on your chest as you 'Mar', and if you concentrate, you'll also feel the vibration on the top of your head. Don't worry about doing a Tarzan impression; that's the beauty of privacy. What you'll discover is the extent of your upper chest resonating chamber, and its effect is impressive.

Persevere with discovering the vibration at the top of your skull. It's not terribly dramatic, but it is important. Engaging with your resonators naturally amplifies your sound without stress or strain, and will make your voice carry and fill the space. Experiment with moving your hands around the top of your head as you vary the pitch and volume of your 'Mar'.

This exercise is helpful if you're concerned that you sound too nasal when you speak, something I hear a lot from my clients. If you're not sure, pinch your nose as you're in full 'Mar' mode, and if the sound changes significantly, then you're working your nasal cavity, which isn't your best resonator. The fix is equally simple: take a breath in the normal way, but hold your nose as you start your 'Mar', and after a few seconds, let go. You'll hear the difference when your sound is free to roam around your natural amplifiers.

So far, we've only worked on one range of movement, and we need to complete the jaw and lip workout by adding these sounds:

- **Mee** – a really cheesy smile helps get into position with the stretch in the horizontal plane

- **May** – the midway compromise between the two, equal height and width

- **More** – same shape, but with thicker lips as they pucker up

- **Moo** – the other extreme, lips fully pursed, with hardly room for your index finger

I demonstrate how to transition from Mee to Moo in the video at www.myfirsttrainers.com

You can join these nonsensical sounds together: 'Mar-More-Mee-May-Moo' is my favourite sequence because I can feel the work my jaw and lips need to do to go from one sound to another. However, you need to claim this as your own My Business Voice Methodology®, so feel free to work out what works best for you and have some fun varying the speed, volume, pitch and tone.

That's all there is to my five-minute Low Drama No Excuse Warm-up. Make time to do this for your next presentation or high-stakes meeting and you'll give yourself a head start.

The objective of the 'Translating Theory Into Practice And Performance' section of my book is to give you 'complete piece of mind'. This is not a typing error, but a deliberate reference to the two sides of your brain. One demands sound logic and theory, backed up by robust research and observational evidence. The other needs practical application and connection to your emotional responses.

I've given you examples and exercises that will turn the reflective work you've done in the previous sections into something useful in the real world of work. This is only the start, and is intended to be the catalyst for your new communication chemistry, where you'll have the confidence to experiment with different solutions to stubborn challenges. This is the very essence of my work in helping my clients unlock their business voices and become confident enough to try different approaches to get to their goals.

In the final section, I'll take you through how to keep going, celebrate your small wins and embed what you've achieved into the best business voice for you. That is how the new you becomes the normal you.

CHAPTER 12

You With Added Skills And Techniques

This final section serves a dual purpose. If you're reading the book for the first time, it will become your call to action. If you're revisiting, it's a permanent reminder not only to review how you're getting on, but also to motivate yourself to think about what to look at next. My recommendation is that you read this section again in three months' time to remind yourself of the core concepts we've worked on and provide an overall context for unlocking your business voice in the continually changing modern world of work.

While digital disruption is much talked about by business leaders, what's perhaps less obvious is the necessity of disruptive voices to make technology work for everyone. Now is the right time for you to move out of the 'echo-verse' and to embrace the next 'dare to be different' phase of your career. The last lap bell has sounded, so go for the line.

Let me help you unlock your business voice once and for all.

For years, I believed that great business leaders and entrepreneurs accumulated their knowledge and expertise by reading vast libraries of personal development books. This was recently challenged by my mentor, Daniel Priestley, who is himself an entrepreneur, bestselling author and accomplished public speaker. I had the privilege to work with Daniel on his Key Person of Influence accelerator programme for emerging entrepreneurs and learnt a great deal from both him and his team at Dent.

His insight into entrepreneurial success is based on his many years of working globally with high-achieving business leaders and the fact that they place emphasis on a few key principles, focusing on refining the specifics that work for them. That means they remain curious about the wider issues, but never forget to revisit the things that really make a difference to their business. This is how extremely busy people manage their personal development, thereby avoiding spreading their precious time too thinly.

That's why unlocking your business voice must be a significant component of your business success story. I'll now remind you of what we've unlocked so far, encourage you to celebrate your wins (small and large), and if you have the odd fail, reposition that as an allowable 'First Attempt In Learning'.

What's in a name?

Nobody likes to fail, and there's one issue that my clients bring up which they say makes them break out into a cold sweat. That issue is remembering people's names when they meet a new group. The sense of panic is a sure-fire way to make them clam up and lock their important voice away, even before they get started.

Here is another quick win you can use from the get-go that I've learnt from a friend and colleague. He's brilliant at remembering people's names – on the many occasions I've worked with him, I've seen that his workshops will have more than thirty participants, and somehow he can remember everyone's name.

I asked him once how he did it, and his response was, 'Because I'm not good at remembering names, so I've made a conscious effort to find a way.' This epitomises my belief that everyone can unlock their business voice, even if they regard themselves as naturally introverted and reflective. It's purely a matter of finding what works for you and committing to making it personal for you.

My colleague's top three tips for when he meets somebody for the first time are:

- 💬 **Be present** – take a breath and focus on that person only
- 💬 **Use it or lose it** – find a reason to repeat their name back to them, even if it's just to check you've got it right

165

💬 **Context** – connect another piece of information to their name, e.g. where they've travelled from or where they work, etc.

The first time I used these tips was at a prestigious business school, and instead of 'Be present' I wrote 'Focus' as the first point on the flipchart. By the time I'd finished the second point, 'Use it or lose it', I realised I'd rather sealed my fate in terms of the acronym I was about to create for the students by finishing with 'Context'. It turned out OK; I didn't blink, apologise, or draw too much attention to the flip chart. A simple final comment of 'And that completes the easy three-step process to remembering names,' got me out of gaol.

The revised acronym 'BUC' exemplifies what you'll be doing: 'bucking the trend' by remembering people's names when you first meet them. I'm always amazed how impressed people are when you do. It makes an immediate impact on the person you're meeting for the first time, really adds to your authority and increases your confidence right away.

Over time and as your career progresses, the five stages of the My Business Voice Methodology® will change. Because you own it, you'll need to revisit it.

Here's why you need to repeat the VOICE prescription.

Your audience will change over time

You may already have experienced the transient nature of teams at work. Just as you're getting used to one set of colleagues and their ways of working, it's time to move on to something else. Add to that the more fluid movement of technical skills across business sectors, and you can easily find yourself working with stakeholders who have different needs and ways of communicating, even when the technical requirements of the job remain the same.

A good example of this is a client of mine who started his career as a Systems Engineer and then got promoted to Head of IT Delivery at an international corporate law firm. There was a natural progression to this type of work, and my client made a smooth transition from fixing problems to future-proofing his company from the changing demands of the industry. His technical expertise was never in doubt, but my client now needed to influence people at senior partner level, and he needed to be quick. After all, these people charge by the minute.

A common mistake he made was trying to condense 100 minutes of content into ten when asked to present at Senior Stakeholders meetings. I worked with him to change the starting point for his ten minutes from a 'walk through of the system' to why it mattered and how it would directly benefit the law practice. This didn't take up the full slot he'd been afforded on the agenda, but it gave his colleagues the critical insight they needed at the time, with the option to explore the specific details then or at another time.

By the way, giving back some time to the frequently over-crowded agendas of Senior Management meetings is a fantastic way to make a good impression.

Your depth of knowledge diminishes as your bandwidth increases

As your career progresses, your exposure across the business increases and more people get to see you and know how you operate. That's a good thing, because the number of people who know and value you is directly proportional to the influence you'll have.

There is an opposite dynamic to this that you may have already experienced. Clients often tell me that this phenomenon creeps up on them, and it can be a shock when they're first exposed as not knowing the answer to a question right away, when previously they've enjoyed and even revelled in their depth of knowledge of projects and initiatives. If you ever feel a bit deflated when this happens to you, remember that university professors accept that the smartest person in their lectures, in terms of knowledge, is any student with a smartphone.

Treat this as good news and make it work for you. This is the time to reframe your value as an expert from merely having the relevant knowledge to sharing your insights and opinions. You still need to be willing to add the context and headlines in your area of expertise; the trick to unlocking your business voice, however, is to take a risk and be disruptive with your views. This is your business voice, unlocked.

As a final reminder, here is the five-step combination to unlocking your business VOICE:

- **Vocation** – be clear that communication is a hard (not soft) skill that helps you do your job

- **Observation** – learn from others and distil what works for you in different situations
- **Intention** – choose to have an effect on your audience rather than just download content
- **Casting** – stretch your comfort zone within the boundaries of the authentic you
- **Experiment** – try things out and aim for different rather than perfect outcomes

Celebrate small wins and accept the occasional fail

The most cynical person you'll never meet is your inner monologue. Even when you start with good intentions, unless you're specific about what you want to achieve from the process of unlocking your business voice, it'll convince you that it's not worth the effort.

The antidote is simple and involves the courage to set your own target for unlocking your business voice. Here are some examples my clients set themselves prior to meetings and presentations:

- Hook my stakeholder with the headline and see how much of the detail I need to offer before getting their buy-in/decision
- Reframe building rapport from worrying about making small talk to being intellectually curious about others' viewpoints and experiences

169

- Jump in and offer an early opinion in the meeting, before reflecting on all the variables and following where the discussion goes as a result

The trick to setting these targets is little and often, over a short but sustained period. You will make faster progress if you focus on one thing at a time for a couple of weeks and then have a break. The most crucial step is to reflect equally on what works and what could have gone better.

Professionals in personal development refer to a 'FAIL' as a First Attempt In Learning, and I encourage you to do the same. Equally important is to celebrate your small wins, and this will only happen if you create a routine for yourself.

My recommendation is to record a message to your cynical inner monologue on your smartphone immediately after your target meeting, presentation or event. Make it short, and stick to saying how you performed against your specific target and how it felt. Be objective and imagine you're talking to yourself in a couple of weeks' time, when your confidence will be lower than now. I am often surprised at how much I have forgotten when I listen back to or watch what I've previously recorded, even after only a few days.

Don't get burdened by this routine; discipline yourself to try it for a couple of weeks at a time, then take a break and reflect on what you've discovered. You'll know when it's right to do it again because your awareness of how you communicate and the impact you have on others will be on the up.

Unlocking your VOICE in the digital age

The digital age has well and truly arrived for everyone and the future is already here, although not evenly distributed. The impact on business and the working world is significant and will only increase. Human Resources leaders (now often referred to as 'Heads of People') know that everyone will need new skills and behaviours going forward. Talent wars have already started in Silicon Valley.

For any organisation, the opposing force to progress is resistance to change, and many people are experiencing the discomfort of having to relearn how to learn. Social media practices have infiltrated the workplace, with more and more people 'working out loud' and sharing micro peer reviews with their community. As a result, social contracts are increasingly becoming more important than formal agreements as the way people work evolves with technology.

At the turn of the twenty-first century, robots started building cars and manual workers had to adapt and develop new skills and behaviours. Now it's the turn of knowledge workers as artificial intelligence will automate many traditionally white-collar jobs.

So what will actually be left for humans to do and achieve?

What's left is what makes us quintessentially human; that is, the ability to persuade our fellow human beings by listening and collecting a variety of differing views and opinions, empathising with everyone, and reaching out to colleagues who haven't had the benefits of our

171

research or insights. Finally, we continually need to lead each other in the pursuit of new and innovative ways of achieving our goals. All of which will require us to have a confident and unlocked business voice to keep up with the ever-increasing rate of progress which technology is driving forward.

Far from being something to be worried about, this brave new world is tremendously exciting and arguably will help us to evolve and fulfil our potential as human beings. Play your part and bring your business voice into the arena. You've always had a VOICE; now it's time to turn up the dial.

I have an immense sense of satisfaction when I see my clients making small but significant changes to their communication style, and the huge benefits they get from persevering with the work and coming back to it as and when they need to. Not everyone has it in them to succeed, and their true business voices remain locked away. On the rare occasions I've seen people who are simply not cut out for the business lives they aspire to, it's made me want to understand why this can happen. It's something I've brought up with my peers and other coaches I respect, and we're all drawn to the same conclusion.

People who simply can't unlock their business voices fall prey to listening too intently to their critics, and one critic in particular – themselves. This would be my biggest warning to you. You won't make progress if you give in to your inner monologue. It's important to pay attention to it, but it's never a good idea to put it solely in charge of your actions.

Your inner critic is the unlocked version of your inner monologue. It's much louder and a lot more persuasive, and will make you take refuge, 'locked away' in a safe place in the belief that you're fine as you are. While this is true in some respects, there is a limit to where accumulating knowledge and expertise can get you.

In order to move forward and gain the influence and status you deserve, take a few risks and move out of your comfort zone. This isn't easy because the voice of the inner critic is so potent; it traps you in the limitations of the here and now rather than letting you imagine a better future.

At the beginning of our journey together, I highlighted some of the frustrations that you can experience when your business voice is locked down. Now that we've discussed your combination to unlocking your business voice, here's the reverse of those frustrations and what you can look forward to:

- I find it easy to speak up and share my ideas in discussions and meetings
- My voice sounds as clear and confident out loud as it does in my head
- Other people get hooked quickly and often say, 'Tell me more about that'
- My confidence levels remain the same when I'm challenged on my views

173

💬 The status and intent behind my message is chosen and driven by me

I often close my workshops with a poem taken from Theodore Roosevelt's 'Citizenship in a Republic' speech, delivered at the Sorbonne in Paris in 1910. It is the best way I know of silencing your inner critic. Please take inspiration from it, as I have done over the years.

It is not the critic who counts;

Not the man who points out where the strong man stumbled, or where the doer of deeds could have done them better.

The credit belongs to the man who is actually in the arena,

Whose face is marred by dust and sweat and blood;

Who strives valiantly;

Who errs, who comes short again and again...

Who knows great enthusiasms...

Who at the best knows in the end the triumph of high achievement,

And who at the worst, if he fails, at least fails while daring greatly,

So that his place shall never be with those cold and timid souls who neither know victory nor defeat.

Almost three decades ago, when I started work, my father gave me the 'It's not just what you know, but who you know' tutorial. For my son, who's now nearly the same age as I was then, I would amend that to 'It's not just what you know, but how you're known'.

I truly believe that your best version of yourself, with added skill and technique, will always be good enough. That is the way for you to be known by others.

Now go and unlock your business voice!

Acknowledgements

To my wife Alicia and children Jack and Alexandria for always keeping me grounded and inspiring me to be a better human being.

To Jonny for not hanging up immediately every time I open a call with *'I've got a great idea'*.

To Marien for that early and humbling lesson on leaving your own ego at the workshop door.

To James, my ex-boss turned friend and now Chairman, for his unrelenting support and iron fist in a velvet glove approach to keeping me on course.

To Julia and my friends at 'The Bakehouse' for their faith and trust over the years and helping me grow and love what I do. www.iopenerinstitute.com

To Linda for being the best agent a middle-aged rookie actor could wish for. www.apmassociates.net

To Moyra, Mat and Paul for taking a leap of faith with my creativity. www.mercuri.co.uk

To Shirley and Judith for so many memorable moments in the training room. www.develop-global.com

To Sandra and Julie for sharing the journey to great things and finding a place for me along the way. www.theartofwork.uk.com

And last but certainly not least, to all my awesome clients and students who have shared their challenges and shown amazing courage in working on them.

The Author

During nearly thirty years in business, Simon de Cintra has coached and mentored subject matter experts who've needed to make more of an impact. Although Simon started his career in sales, the defining moment came when he left the corporate world behind and, in his late thirties, joined the Actors Company to train professionally as an actor. On his arrival at drama school, the early criticism of *'stop acting'* and *'beautifully said, didn't believe a word'*, inspired him to seek the formula behind truthful and authentic communication.

On graduating from drama school, he set up MyFirstTrainers® and for over ten years, has delivered workshops and coaching sessions all over the world for leading business schools and in private and public sector businesses.

What Simon discovered from working with thousands of technical experts is that everybody's best version of themselves is good enough; it's not about having to be an actor, it's about being comfortable in your own voice and making it work for you. He has combined his understanding of the corporate world with his experience as a jobbing actor to design a book for people looking to improve their influence at work. In *Unlock Your Business Voice*, Simon describes a simple framework for finding your most impactful business voice in the fast-growing world of high tech business.

Simon's simple mantra is *'Make what you say count to the people that matter'*.

To find out more about Simon's work, visit www.myfirsttrainers.com

You can connect with Simon on LinkedIn and on Twitter @MyFirstTrainers

Printed in Great Britain
by Amazon